SO-AYT-495

The State of
Black Fort Wayne

**Fort Wayne Urban League
227 E. Washington Blvd.
Fort Wayne, Indiana 46803**

**Henry O. Hall • Chairman
A. V. Fleming, D.B.A. • President & CEO**

Published by
The Fort Wayne Urban League
2003

NATIONAL URBAN LEAGUE

The nation's oldest and largest community-based movement empowering African Americans to enter the economic and social mainstream.

The National Urban League is proud to endorse Fort Wayne Urban League's first *State of Black Fort Wayne* publication. Subtitled, "A Statistical Profile of the African American Community," this timely publication provides important information on topical areas such as demographics, education, employment, business and economic development, housing, poverty and crime, justice, and health.

These are challenging times for our communities as we continue the struggle for social, political and economic equity. Federal funds to help develop and strengthen our communities are rapidly shrinking; public schools that have educated generations of the Black community are at risk and as such are failing to provide our children with the quality education they deserve.

These are just a couple of the challenges we face in these early years of the 21st century. The *State of Black Fort Wayne* statistically captures the reality of the Black community in this part of Indiana. More importantly, it provides a valuable resource for community members and decision-makers alike, who are committed to working together to effect meaningful change. We congratulate you on your accomplishment.

Best regards,

Marc H. Morial
President & CEO
National Urban League

FORT WAYNE URBAN LEAGUE

The State of Black Fort Wayne takes on special relevance at a time when many communities around the United States are using cultural differences as a strategy for economic development, inclusiveness, and improving the quality of life for all citizens involved. The African American community must begin a process of self-evaluation of the state in which we live. It is through this process, that we can begin to truly comprehend and understand the extent of our power, strengths, and weaknesses. The information in the State of Black Fort Wayne is comprised of eight chapters: Demographics, Housing, Employment, Poverty, Business and Economic Development, Education, Crime and Justice, and Health. These chapters cover a wide range of subject matter that influence the African American community. Local professionals examined secondary research that will give both practitioners and laypersons a snapshot of how African-Americans influence and shape our community. Further, this will be the first time in many years that there will be one source of information available with a wide variety of topics concerning African Americans in Fort Wayne. The Fort Wayne Urban League will use this information to continue to carry out its mission and increase its role in the area of Education, Economic Development, Parity and Power and Civil Rights. It is our belief that the information and the interpretation by the writers will give the community a better understanding of both the challenges and obstacles facing African Americans in the city of Fort Wayne.

Sincerely,

Dr. A.V. Fleming
President & CEO
Fort Wayne Urban League

SPECIAL NOTE OF THANKS TO JOHN DICKMEYER:

The Fort Wayne Urban League would like to extend special thanks to John Dickmeyer, Business Specialist with the Allen County Public Library. Mr. Dickmeyer was extremely instrumental in gathering much of the data utilized by the writers in producing the State of Black Fort Wayne document. Without Mr. Dickmeyer's patience and assistance, this project would have been impossible to complete.

ACKNOWLEDGEMENTS:

Many other persons also gave generously of their time and expertise in bringing this document to fruition. They include:

- The writers of the various chapters: Shayne Abrahams, Andy J. Barrett, Ruby Cain, Dr. C. K. Chauhan, John Cuellar, Andy Downs, Sherri Emerson, Dr. A.V. Fleming, Dr. Shirley Hollis, Verleaish Jones, Dr. Ronald L. Mize, Jonathan C. Ray, Greg Smith, Dr. Thomas D. Stucky, and Jeff Vaughn;

- The editors of the draft chapters: Dr. Jeanette Clausen, Dr. Pamela Jordan, Dr. Richard Ramsey, Yvonne Ramsey, and Dr. Matt Smith;

- Fort Wayne city planners: Dennis Donahue and John Urbahns, who produced the maps;

- Scott Bent and Ann Newsom, who provided guidance in layout and production of the document;

- Tamyra Kelly and the United Way of Allen County, who provided assistance in getting the document printed;

- Fort Wayne Urban League Bridging the Gap Committee members: Thomas Black, Carol Cartwright, Dr. Miles Edwards, Reverend William Gary, Sondra Mergenthal and Carl Stephens, who provided helpful comments and critiques of the draft document;

- Ramona McGown, coordinator of the State of Black Fort Wayne project, and

- Fort Wayne Urban League Board of Directors.

We and the community owe a tremendous debt of gratitude to all of them for persisting through many months to produce a quality finished product.

 **National Urban League Affiliate**

FORT WAYNE URBAN LEAGUE

 **Affiliated Agency United Way of Allen County**

Officers

HENRY O. HALL, CHAIRMAN
NATIONAL CITY BANK

COZEY BAKER, TREASURER
FOUNTAINHEAD ADVISORS, LLC

DAVITA MITCHELL, SECRETARY
INDIANA REGIONAL MINORITY
DEVELOPMENT COUNCIL

DR. A.V. FLEMING
PRESIDENT & CEO

Members

WILL CLARK
RETIRED

DR. JEANETTE CLAUSEN
IPFW

DR. DOUGLAS COUTTS
FT. WAYNE COMMUNITY SCHOOLS

DAVID DONELLY
BANK ONE

ELLEN FELTS
WELLS FARGO

CARMEN FILES
SUPERIOR ESSEX

TIA WALKER
BUSINESS & EDUCATION CONSULTANT

REV. WILLIAM GARY
TURNER CHAPEL A.M.E.

KAREN GOINS
INTERNATIONAL HARVESTER

JAMES GRAHAM
MAPLE GROVE COMMUNITY CENTER

KENNETH KNIGHT
GENERAL MOTORS

CYNTHIA MCBRIDE
SMALL BUSINESS CENTER

TERRY O'NEIL
BANK ONE

DOUG RICE
FT. WAYNE NEWSPAPERS

BRIAN STILES
ROTHBERG, LOGAN & WARSCO

KELLIE TURNER
21ST CENTURY SCHOLARS

NICOLE TURNER-ABRAHAMS
FWUL GUILD PRESIDENT
PROJECT RENEW

DR. MICHAEL WARTELL
IPFW

SUSAN WESNER
BADEN, GAGE & SCHROEDER

KELLY ZACHRICH
SUPER SHOT

BRIDGING THE GAP COMMITTEE

REV. WILLIAM GARY • CHAIR
SONDRA MERGENTHAL • THOMAS BLACK • DR. MILES EDWARDS

FORT WAYNE URBAN LEAGUE STAFF

DR. A.V. FLEMING
PRESIDENT & CEO

Program/Research Director
Carol Cartwright

Marketing Consultant
Maye Johnson

Seniors in Community Service Director
DeCarlo Wallace-Winfield

Director of Education and Youth Development
Joe Shade Jr.

Finance Director
Etse Mulugeta

Bridging the Gap Coordinator
Ramona McGown

Seniors in Community Service Counselor
Delania Ayers

Capital Campaign Grant Writer
Jasjit Bahl

Bookkeeper
Leola Jones

Campaign for African American Achievement Coordinator
Carl Stephens

Seniors in Community Service
Carlotta Cochran   June Erby
Rudolph Bennett   Thomas Mickles
Tennie Bynum   Leonia Williams
Vianna Sims

Capital Campaign Fundraising Consultant
John Dize

Employment & Training Director
Richard Espinosa

Parent Involvement Coordinator
Adrienne Jackson

Economic Development Coordinator
Ramona Chapman

Employment Specialist
Leon Gondell

Urban Enterprise Zone Coordinator
Rufus Hamilton

Pontiac Youth Center Coordinator
Veronica Wormbly

Mission Statement:

The mission of the Fort Wayne Urban League is to enable African Americans and others to secure economic self-reliance, parity, and power and civil rights.

Chapter 1: Demographics

Andy Downs

INTRODUCTION

Between 1990 and 2000, Fort Wayne grew by more than 32,000 people (19%). As it grows, Fort Wayne is becoming more diverse. In 1990, almost 80% of the population was White. By 2000, that percentage had dropped to less than 75%. The Hispanic population experienced the largest growth among minorities (7,358 people). African-Americans were the largest minority group in 1990 (16.6% of the population) and are still the largest minority group in 2000 (17.1% of the population). The African-American population grew by more than 6,500 people between 1990 and 2000. That growth made up one-third of the growth of minorities.

There are two primary differences between the age distributions of the Fort Wayne population and the African-American population. The first is that the African-American population has a much larger percentage of its population younger than 10 years of age. The second is that the Fort Wayne population has a much larger percentage of its population over the age of 65. A further examination of the population age distribution shows that the African-American and White populations have remained fairly stable. For the African-American population, White population, and Fort Wayne population, the largest growth came in the 40 to 49 year old group. The largest drop was in the 30 to 39 year old group. The greatest growth in the Hispanic population was in the 20 to 29 year old group (18.7% to 25.6%).

The median household income for the African-American population still trails behind the median for the population as a whole, Whites, and Hispanics. In 1999, the greatest difference was between the African-American population and the White population ($11,186). Fortunately there has been some improvement between 1989 and 1999.

Table 3. Median Household Income, 1999

Median Household Income, 1999	
Total Population	$36,518
White	$38,399
African Americans	$27,213
Hispanic	$34,342

Source: United States Bureau of the Census Summary File 3

KEY FINDINGS

- Minorities make up 27 % of Fort Wayne's Population.

- The percentage of African-Americans with less than a high school education has dropped from 36% to 24%.

- Thirty-nine percent of African-Americans lived in a household with an income of at least $35,000.

- The percentage of African-Americans living below the poverty line has remained stable.

Table 1. Population by Race for 1990 and 2000.

	1990	Percent of the Population in 1990	2000	Percent of the Population in 2000	Population Growth from 1990 to 2000
Total	173,072	100.0	205,941	100.0	19.0
White	137279	79.3	150,843	73.2	9.9
African American	28708	16.6	35,249	17.1	22.8
Hispanic	4394	2.5	11,752	5.7	167.5
American Indian, Eskimo, or Aleut	604	0.3	690	0.3	14.2
Asian or Pacific Islander	1712	1.0	3,106	1.5	81.4
Other race	375	0.2	4301	2.1	1046.9

Source: United States Bureau of the Census Summary Tape File 3

Table 2. Population by Race and Age for 1990 and 2000.

	1990								2000							
	All People	Percent	White	Precent	African Americans	Percent	Hispanic	Percent	All People	Percent	White	Percent	African Amercians	Percent	Hispanic	Percent
9 years or under	26860	15.5	19594	14.1	6015	20.8	1,015	23.1	32,164	15.6	20,758	13.4	7,502	21.1	2,876	24.5
10 to 15 years	13971	8.1	9524	6.9	3897	13.5	580	13.2	17,732	8.6	20277*	13.1	6979*	19.6	1976*	16.8
16 to 19 years	9863	5.7	7213	5.2	2384	8.2	322	7.3	12,157	5.9						
20 to 29 years	30499	17.6	24737	17.8	4681	16.2	821	18.7	32,362	15.7	23,870	15.4	5,270	14.8	3,005	25.6
30 to 39 years	29312	16.9	23660	17.0	4659	16.1	805	18.3	30,449	14.8	23,178	14.9	4,952	13.9	1,823	15.5
40 to 49 years	19114	11.0	15866	11.4	2796	9.7	477	10.9	29,047	14.1	22,647	14.6	5,014	14.1	1,140	9.7
50 to 59 years	13000	7.5	10705	7.7	2032	7.0	113	2.6	19,999	9.7	16,287	10.5	2,664	7.5	583	5.0
60 to 64 years	7220	4.2	6332	4.6	727	2.5	119	2.7	6,514	3.2	5,195	3.3	1,022	2.9	121	1.0
65 years or older	23233	13.4	21374	15.4	1724	6.0	142	3.2	25,517	12.4	22,975	14.8	2,131	6.0	228	1.9
Total	173072	100	139005	100.0	28915	100	4,394	100.0	205,941	100	155,187	100.0	35,534	100	11,752	100.0

* Total for 10 to 19 years

Source: United States Bureau of the Census Summary Tape File 3

The per capita income for Fort Wayne households grew from 1989 to 1999 by almost $5,800. The White population saw the largest growth ($6,547) and the Hispanic population saw the smallest growth ($2,366). The per capita income

that percentage dropped to less than 10% by 2000. For the White population the percentage dropped to less than 8%. For the Hispanic population the percentage dropped to just over 11% and

African-American population still lagged behind the improvements for the population as a whole, the white population, and the Hispanic population. A byproduct of having more than 16% of the Fort Wayne population living in a household with an income of less than $15,000 is a high percentage of people living below the poverty line. In 1990, almost 38% of the Fort Wayne population living below the poverty line were younger than 18. That percentage was lower for the White population (28.9%) and the Hispanic population (36.9%). Between 1990 and 2000, the African-American population saw a slight decrease in the percentage of people younger than 18 living below the poverty line from just over 50% to just under 50%.

Table 4. Per Capita Income, 1989 and 1999

	All people	White	African American	Hispanic
1989 per capita income	12,726	13,792	8,268	8,758
1999 per capita income	18,517	20,339	13,310	11,124
Growth	5,791	6,547	5,042	2,366
Percent growth	45.51	47.47	60.98	27.02

Source: United States Bureau of the Census Summary Tape File 3

of African-Americans in 1989 was $8,268. From 1989 to 1999, the per capita income for the African-American population experienced the largest percentage growth (61%).

for the African-American population it dropped to less than 20%.

In 1990, slightly more than 34% of the Fort Wayne population, slightly more than 35% of the White population, almost

Table 5. Household Income by Income Categories, 1990, and 2000.

	1990								2000							
	All Households	Percent	White	Percent	African Americans	Percent	Hispanic	Percent	All Households	Percent	White	Percent	African Americans	Percent	Hispanic	Percent
Less than $10,000	10,357	14.9	7,809	13.4	2,321	24.8	247	18.1	7,943	9.5	5,004	7.5	2,451	19.2	357	11.3
$10,000 to $14,999	7,012	10.1	5,841	10.0	1,034	11.0	154	11.3	5,613	6.7	4,309	6.5	967	7.6	189	6.0
$15,000 to $24,999	15,314	22.1	12,815	21.9	2,153	23.0	322	23.6	13,334	16.0	10,217	15.4	2,440	19.1	491	15.6
$25,000 to $34,999	12,906	18.6	11,227	19.2	1,360	14.5	239	17.5	12,774	15.3	10,123	15.3	1,974	15.4	564	17.9
$35,000 to $49,999	13,121	18.9	11,366	19.4	1,435	15.3	253	18.6	16,131	19.3	13,210	19.9	1,984	15.5	645	20.5
$50,000 to $74,999	7,982	11.5	7,014	12.0	857	9.1	119	8.7	16,283	19.5	13,908	21.0	1,732	13.5	547	17.4
$75,000 to $99,999	1,603	2.3	1,377	2.4	187	2.0	18	1.3	6,285	7.5	5,297	8.0	644	5.0	252	8.0
$100,000 or more	1,050	1.5	1,008	1.7	23	0.2	10	0.7	5,053	6.1	4,231	6.4	602	4.7	107	3.4
Total	69,345	100	58,457	100.0	9,370	100	1,362	100.0	83,416	100	66,299	100.0	12,794	100	3,152	100.0

Source: United States Bureau of the Census Summary Tape File 3

Another way to evaluate the economic well-being of a population is to look at household income by income categories. In 1990, just under 15% of the Fort Wayne population lived in a household with an income of less than $10,000. Over 13% of the White population, over 18% of the Hispanic population, and almost 25% of the African American population lived in a household with an income of less than $10,000. For the population as a whole,

30% of the Hispanic population, and 26% of the African-American population lived in a household with an income of at least $35,000. In 2000, that number jumped to more than 50% for the population as a whole and for the White population. The Hispanic population experienced an increase to just under 50%. Almost 39% of the African-American population lived in a household with income of at least $35,000. While these improvements are welcomed, the advancements for the

The Fort Wayne population, white population, and Hispanic population all saw increases. The percentage of the population as a whole increased to 39%. The White population increased slightly to 29.1%. The Hispanic population experienced the most dramatic increase to 46.2%

One of the ways to combat poverty is by earning an education. In 1990, over 22% of the Fort Wayne population older than

Table 7. Educational Attainment by Race, 1990 & 2000.

	1990								2000							
	All People	Percent	White	Percent	African Americans	Percent	Hispanic	Percent	All People	Percent	White	Percent	African Americans	Percent	Hispanic	Percent
Less than 9th grade	8,146	7.5	6,106	6.7	1,536	10.7	449	21.6	6,368	5.0	4,008	3.9	1,084	5.9	1,373	25.6
9th to 12th grade, no diploma	16,699	15.4	12,633	13.8	3,585	24.9	382	18.4	15,184	11.9	10,646	10.4	3,352	18.2	1,170	21.8
High school graduate (includes equivalency)	36,371	33.5	31,204	34.0	4,484	31.2	591	28.5	41,939	32.8	33,456	32.6	6,706	36.5	1,495	27.8
Some college, no degree	22,113	20.4	18,772	20.5	3,006	20.9	377	18.2	29,952	23.4	23,985	23.4	4,611	25.1	839	15.6
Associate degree	8,167	7.5	7,240	7.9	771	5.4	127	6.1	9,699	7.6	8,297	8.1	1,085	5.9	177	3.3
Bachelor's degree	11,027	10.2	10,123	11.0	661	4.6	114	5.5	16,521	12.9	14,705	14.3	1,026	5.6	236	4.4
Graduate or professional degree	6,063	5.6	5,587	6.1	328	2.3	35	1.7	8,376	6.5	7,542	7.3	520	2.8	82	1.5
Total	108,586	100.0	91,665	100.0	14,371	100.0	2,075	100.0	128,039	100.0	102,639	100.0	18,384	100.0	5,372	100.0

Source: United States Bureau of the Census Summary Tape File 3

25 years of age had earned less than a high school diploma. The percentage for the white population was just over 20%. The percentage for the African-American population was just over 35% and the Hispanic population was just over 40%. Slightly more than 23% of the Fort Wayne population had earned a college degree. That percentage was just over 25% for the White population, just over 12% for the African-American population, and just over 13% for the Hispanic population.

In 2000, significant improvements had been made in the percentage of people who had earned a high school diploma or more in all populations except the Hispanic population. The percentage of the Hispanic population over 25 years of age who had earned less than a high school diploma jumped to over 47%. The Hispanic population also saw a decrease in the percentage of people with a college degree (9.2%). This is in contrast to the Fort Wayne population (27%), the White population (29.8%), and the African-American population (14.3%) which all saw increases.

Table 8. Total Population in the Southeast Quadrant for 1990 and 2000.

	1990	2000	Change
Total	52368	49878	-2490
White	26317	17368	-8949
African American	24218	27566	3348
Hispanic	1867	4694	2827

Source: United States Bureau of the Census Summary Tape File 3

The maps in this report show that the southeast quadrant of Fort Wayne was the home to the majority of African-Americans in 1990 and still is in 2000. The big difference between 1990 and 2000 has been the increase in the percentage of the total population in the southeast quadrant that is made up of African-Americans. Between 1990 and 2000, the population living in the southeast quadrant decreased 2,490 people. The decrease is due to a reduction in the White population (-8,949). All other racial categories experienced an increase in population in the southeast quadrant. The largest increases were in the Hispanic population (2,827) and the African-American population (3,348).

Fort Wayne has a relatively stable population with over 50% of the population living in the same house in 2000 that they occupied in 1995. For the African-American and White populations, over 83% are either living in the same house or in the same county as they did in 1995. The Hispanic population was the most transient with only 29% of the population living in the same house.

The information in this demographic profile comes from the United States Bureau of the Census *Summary Tape File 3* for the 1990 Census and *Summary File 3* for the 2000 Census. More information can be found at http://factfinder.census.gov.

Table 6. Percent of Individuals Living Below the Poverty Line, 1990 and 2000.

	1990								2000							
	All People	Percent	White	Percent	African Americans	Percent	Hispanic	Percent	All People	Percent	White	Percent	African Americans	Percent	Hispanic	Percent
Under 5 years	1,895	9.7	1,064	9.3	1,312	18.0	64	12.4	3,406	13.5	1,185	9.1	1,516	16.2	486	19.4
5 years	1,013	5.2	180	1.6	238	3.3	16	3.1	669	2.7	274	2.1	293	3.1	114	4.5
6 to 11 years	2,520	12.9	1,224	10.7	1,209	16.6	67	12.9	3,192	12.7	1,301	10.0	1,546	16.5	336	13.4
12 to 17 years	1,895	9.7	836	7.3	1,014	13.9	44	8.5	2,552	10.1	1,033	7.9	1,297	13.8	223	8.9
18 to 64 years	10,213	52.4	6,546	57.4	3,175	43.5	282	54.4	13,586	53.9	8,017	61.5	4,244	45.3	1,300	51.9
65 to 74 years	1,013	5.2	790	6.9	197	2.7	25	4.8	892	3.5	557	4.3	304	3.2	5	0.2
75 years and over	935	4.8	773	6.8	148	2.0	20	3.9	907	3.6	679	5.2	177	1.9	42	1.7
Total	19,484	100.0	11,413	100.0	7,293	100.0	518	100.0	25,204	100.0	13,046	100.0	9,377	100.0	2,506	100.0

Source: United States Bureau of the Census Summary Tape File 3

Table 9. Percent of Population Residing in Same Household.

	All People	Percent	Whites	Percent	African Americans	Percent	Hispanic	Percent
Same house in 1995	96,299	50.7	77,684	53.7	14,378	44.9	2,892	28.8
Different house in 1995	93,475	49.3	66,982	46.3	17,618	55.1	7,146	71.2
in same county	61,481	32.4	44,100	30.5	13,173	41.2	3,094	30.8
in different state	16,295	8.6	11,304	7.8	3,007	9.4	1,941	19.3
Total	189,774		144,666		31,996		10,038	

Source: United States Census Bureau of the Census Summary Tape File 3

Demographics

City of Fort Wayne
1990 African American Population

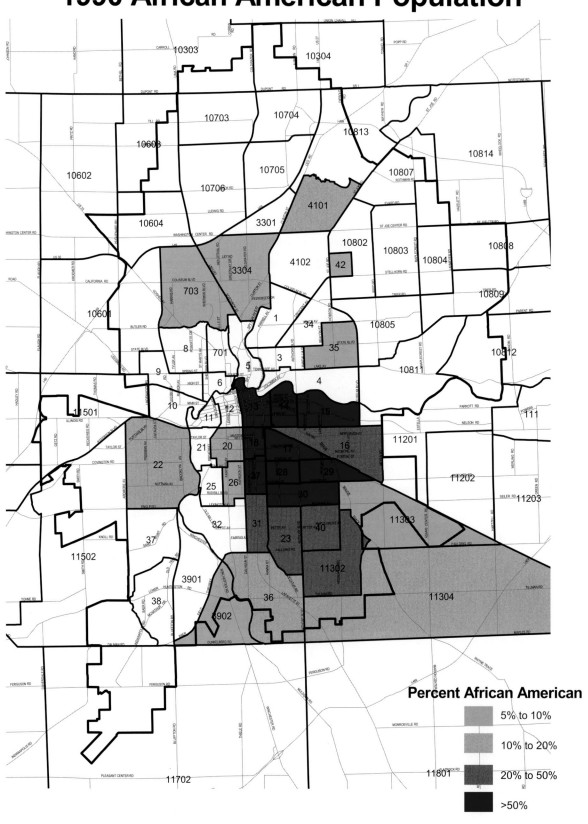

Percent African American

- 5% to 10%
- 10% to 20%
- 20% to 50%
- >50%

The State of Black Fort Wayne • 2003

City of Fort Wayne
2000 African American Population

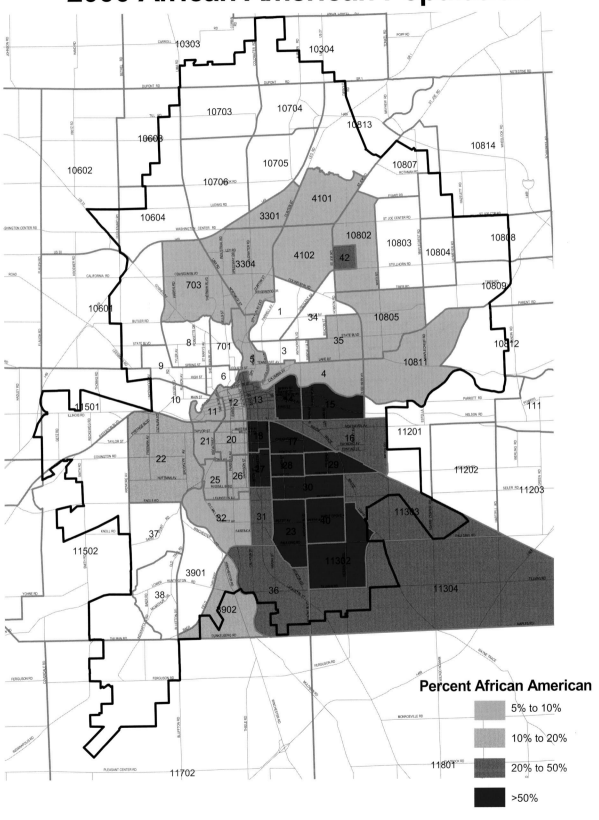

Percent African American

5% to 10%

10% to 20%

20% to 50%

>50%

Chapter 2: Housing

Ronald L. Mize, Ph.D.

INTRODUCTION

This past April commemorated the 35th anniversary of the passage of the Fair Housing Act of 1968. As part of civil rights legislation that arose in response to the unrest caused by the assassination of Dr. Rev. Martin Luther King, Jr., Title VIII of the Civil Rights Act of 1968 (Fair Housing Act) prohibits discrimination in the sale, rental and financing of dwellings based on race, color, religion, sex or national origin. Today, if you look around downtown Fort Wayne in the month of April, banners on street lights proclaim April as "Fair Housing Month," yet no public discussion has taken place on the status of race and housing nor has there been much assessment on the persistence of racial segregation in the Fort Wayne metropolitan area. This is particularly unfortunate when one considers that as of the year 2000, Fort Wayne ranks as the 24th most segregated city in the United States. A 2002 report by ACORN (Association of Community Organizations for Reform Now) found that of the 68 mid-size to large metropolitan US cities they studied, Fort Wayne ranked number one in the percentage rise of rejection rates of African-American home loan applicants. (see Table I in The Acorn Study). Housing segregation impacts every measure of quality of life from livability and health status to access to public and private transportation, high-wage occupations, educational life chances, and interracial relations.

Availability of quality housing stock is certainly part of the larger socio-economic picture so this chapter will briefly discuss the changes in the Fort Wayne local economy as it relates to housing. Then the discussion turns to the current issues in housing that directly impact the Fort Wayne African-American population. Rental concentrations, multi-family unit location, vacancy trends, and residential segregation (both race and class based) are all factors that disproportionately impact Blacks centralized in the southeastern quadrant of the city.

THE SOCIO-ECONOMICS OF HOUSING

The character of the city of Fort Wayne is certainly based in its heavy industry history. How the community is perceived is based on the image of Fort Wayne as a blue-collar, hard-working citizenry. And in fact, the major factories that dominated the city were the first attractors of African Americans to Fort Wayne. International Harvester was one of the first integrated workplaces in the city and recruited a large number of Blacks from Chicago to relocate to its Fort Wayne factory. Housing trends within the city limits tended to be dominated by the burgeoning population who came to Fort Wayne in search of work in its industrial sector. A major transition has defined the current state of

KEY FINDINGS

- Based upon 2000 Census data, approximately 71 percent of Fort Wayne's African-American population would have to relocate to predominately White neighborhoods in order to achieve an integrated residential configuration. This rate of segregation makes Fort Wayne the 24th most segregated city in the United States.

- According to a recent ACORN study of conventional home loan rejection rates, the city with the largest percent increase in the 68 major metropolitan areas they studied was Fort Wayne. In 2000, 30.9 percent of African American home loan applicants were rejected and the number rose to 42.3 percent in 2001 (a 36.7 percent one year increase).

- Low median housing values, high rental concentrations, multi-family unit location, high vacancy trends, are directly related to high residential segregation rates. These quality of life factors disproportionately and negatively impact African-Americans living in the southeastern quadrant of the city.

housing in Fort Wayne but we must examine its prior state in order to understand the contemporary predicament.

The factory town era of housing mimicked the larger social and economic trends of the time. Housing styles became less varied and much more standard and uniform. Fort Wayne increasingly became dependent on large-scale industrial production. Like many other urban centers of the Midwest, Fort Wayne entered into the *factory town* phase of housing trends that lasted into the early 1980's. The city appeared much more homogenous in its attempt to provide housing quickly for the workers of the booming industrial economy. As large factories tended to dominate particular sections of the city, shotgun houses were quickly constructed in the immediate, surrounding area to house the workers. Typically, homes were either built in the same A-frame or single level ranch styles. As early as 1927, the factory town began to solidify its existence in Fort Wayne.

A story by John Clark ran on September 10, 1927 in the *Saturday Evening Post* and explained the link between housing and industrial development.

Fort Wayne, Indiana, prior to 1920 was an average small city; a division point on the Pennsylvania's main line and plant of the General Electric Company its mainstay. In 1920 the city went after the new plant of the International Harvester Company and won it fairly in warm competition with twenty other cities. The Greater Fort Wayne Corporation, with a capital of $1,000,000…was formed primarily to build homes for the harvester company's employees; but private enterprise took care of this, it was found, and the body turned its energies to attracting other industries.

International Harvester eventually employed over 10,000 workers. The wire industry established its base of operations in Fort Wayne and during various times of the factory town phase, the supply of wire from Fort Wayne constituted 50 and 90 percent of magnet wire and wire-die produced in the US. Beyond heavy industry, Fort Wayne also became strongly represented in the area of financial services. With the Lincoln National firms and other financial service providers, up until 1997 Fort Wayne ranked 10th in terms of assets among the US's top ten largest insurance company cities. But the financial sector was one of the few Fort Wayne industries that was able to stave off, until quite recently, the effects of current trends.

The current phase of *deindustrialization* is part of a larger trend in the urban Midwest and Northeast where the factory town presided. As a result of shifts in the US economy away from manufacturing and more towards service-based industries, we find that this substantially impacts the housing market. For instance, occupations in the high-end of the new economy include computer programming, new information technologies and services, biotechnology, and high-tech. research/development yield high incomes and demand for expensive single-family homes. Low-wage service sector jobs in hospitality, food service, healthcare, and retail tend to rarely allow employees to afford such amenities.

For the most part, service sector jobs in the Midwest have tended to follow the low-wage trend (see Table I). This should serve as a point of concern given the fact that the service industry is currently the largest sector employer in the state of Indiana.

From 1991 to 2001, Indiana has witnessed a significant shift in the distribution of employment

Table I. Percent of Net Job Growth/Decline in Midwest, 1963-1986.

Earnings per year (in 1985 constant dollars)	1963-1973	1973-1979	1979-1986
Lowest Stratum (less than $11,104)	-5.2	16.5	96.0
Middle Stratum ($11,104-44,412)	81.4	80.8	-4.8
High Stratum (more than $44,412)	23.8	2.7	8.8

Adapted from: Dudley (1994) p.35 and Harrison and Bluestone (1988) Appendix 2A.

between sectors. Employment in the service sector increased by 40%, followed by a 35% gain in construction and an 18% increase in wholesale and retail trade. During this period, the number of manufacturing jobs also increased by 3%. However, manufacturing jobs declined from a 24.7% share of total non-farm employment to a 21.7% share. The service sector increased from 21.5% to 25.7%, and is now the largest single sector of employment in Indiana.

Job growth in the entire Midwest has been almost exclusively in the low-wage portion of the economy. Middle stratum jobs declined for the first time in the 1980's and the earlier trends of middle stratum predominance and significant high stratum increases have come to an end. The demand for expensive housing is severely limited by the lack of new high-wage job creation. Homeownership also becomes a lofty, and at times unattainable goal, with new job creation occurring almost exclusively at the lowest stratum.

Other issues that have arisen in the deindustrialization phase are the coupled processes of suburban sprawl and White flight. The downtown commercial centers have tended to fade as suburban shopping malls and strip malls dominate on the outskirts of the city. In Fort Wayne, most of the new home building (84 percent) has occurred outside the city limits of Fort Wayne from the period of 1996 to 1999. New commercial growth has also been limited to the southwest and northern sections of the Fort Wayne

metropolitan area. In many of the recently coined 'rust belt' cities, urban experts have recognized the trend of an abandonment of the central city. Zones marked for industrial use often fall into disrepair and disuse as the formerly well-paying factory jobs are relocated in the name of competitive advantage. Rust belt factories are often vacant shells of their former selves as firms downsize or relocate operations. This has a major impact on the surrounding communities that often housed the workers of those factories. Those individuals who can afford to flee the central cities of the Midwest often leave behind neighborhoods that are segregated racially and socioeconomically. Current efforts at downtown revitalization must take this situation into account when developing feasible plans and new growth strategies.

CURRENT ISSUES FACING THE FORT WAYNE HOUSING MARKET

There are a number of issues currently facing the Fort Wayne housing market. The recently commissioned "City of Fort Wayne Housing Market Study and Development Strategy" covers quite adequately the issues of the existing housing market, potential demand for future housing, and situation of Southeast Fort Wayne. In addition to those issues, there are both overlapping and additional areas of concern in regards to the current housing situation. A major issue is the demographic distribution of the African-American population in the six largest townships that comprise 87.5 percent of Allen County's population and the accompanying

median property values of those townships. The second issue is the differential rates of owner occupied versus tenancy in particular sectors within the city limits. A third issue is the location and prevalence of multi-family units in relation to single-family houses. A fourth issue that relates specifically to the city of Fort Wayne is the status of vacant, often times certifiable tax delinquent, properties and the process whereby the city government is able to remedy, demolish, or resell those dwellings. The final issue is racial segregation in housing, which was the express target of the 1968 Fair Housing Act. Social scientists find that our current rates of segregation are at an all-time high in the history of our nation. In addition, segregation along socio-economic lines is also highly prevalent. We find that both issues are directly relevant to Fort Wayne and its surrounding communities.

ALLEN COUNTY TOWNSHIP DATA AND MEDIAN HOUSING VALUES

The population of Allen County is 331,849 and is divided into twenty townships. The six townships that account for 290,430 residents (87.5 percent) are St. Joe, Perry, Aboite, Adams, Washington, and Wayne. In the suburban townships of Aboite, Perry, Saint Joe, and Washington; only 3.3 percent of their residents are African-American. Wayne Township has the largest number and percentage of African-American residents with 23,931 or 22 percent of the township's population. Looking at median housing values by township, one finds that White-dominated townships have the highest median housing value whereas the median housing value of Wayne Township ($59,200) is 40% of the average home value in Perry Township ($147,900).

TENANCY VS. OWNER OCCUPIED ISSUES

Areas with significant rates of rental occupied units are subject to a set of conditions rarely associated with owner-occupied areas. Issues of upkeep, absentee landlords, transience of the population, lack of community/neighborly ties, and a high rate of multi-family housing are specific to high rental-occupied areas. Given the comparatively affordable housing market, it is highly likely that anyone who wishes to own could find a home in their price range. Due to the incredibly low cost of properties in Fort Wayne, it is often the case, particularly in detached single-family dwellings, that rental rates exceed the amount tenants would pay on a mortgage should they own their dwelling. When examining the distribution of renter-occupied units in Fort Wayne, one finds they tend to be concentrated. These rental-dominated tracts are found in the central part of the city and its immediate surroundings. High rates of owner-occupied units are found on the outskirts of the city and in predominately white neighborhoods. Map I shows the percentage of renter occupied units.

Overall, the highest concentrations of renter-occupied units are in the central city and its immediate surrounding tracts. High renter concentrations can also be found to the north, east, and southeast of downtown. The only high rates of owner-occupied units are in the northeast and northwest portions of the city. Pockets of owner-occupancy can also be found in a segment of the southwest and far southeast quadrants.

SINGLE FAMILY VS. MULTI-FAMILY ISSUES

The issues that arise from the concentration of multi-family or single-family housing units are also closely related to the nature of racial and socioeconomic segregation patterns. The overall pattern found in the city of Fort Wayne is a concentration of multi-family unit housing in the center of the city and its immediate surroundings in all four directions. Single-family housing concentration is found on the outskirts of the city. Map II represents the census tracts with multi-family detached structures exceeding 40 percent. The center of the city includes a high concentration of non-single-family detached structures.

Multi-family units can represent very mixed results in terms of their effects on other housing stock in the area. In terms of a judicious use of space, multi-family units often serve the function of housing a large number of people in a comparatively small confine. If community parks or open spaces are part of an overall plan in the development and maintenance of multi-unit housing, the shared use of living space, adjoining walls, and a resultant feeling of crowding can be mitigated. Multi-family unit housing most often is tenant occupied but various housing trends in other parts of the US are moving toward owner occupied multi-unit family structures. Multi-family units that attempt to maximize the number of tenants, regardless of space constraints, or do not offer amenities to mitigate the shared space concerns have an overall effect of deteriorating the neighborhood with high transience rates and low quality of living.

VACANCY RATES AND CERTIFIABLE TAX DELIQUENT PROPERTIES

The existence of vacant lots and housing structures has a particularly detrimental impact on local neighborhoods. According to the 2001 <u>Housing Market Study and Development Strategy</u> report,

vacant lots break up the community fabric and have a negative impact on the overall image of the neighborhood. In addition, however, they offer opportunities for in-fill development, especially those lots that can be grouped together to form large development parcels.

So vacant lots not only represent the most visible signs of urban decay and disinvestment but also the opportunity for redevelopment and neighborhood improvement. In addition, high levels of vacancy are extremely strongly correlated with African-American concentrated neighborhoods ($r = .655$, $p < 01$). Map III show the percentage of vacant housing units in each tract, but the results can be summarized that the census tracts with greater than 20 percent vacant housing units (tracts 14, 17 and 18) are located near the central and southeast sections of the city. They are also some of the most concentrated tracts of African-American residents. Tract 14 is 69 percent, tract 17 is 81.27 percent (the highest neighborhood concentration in the city), and tract 18 is 68.39 percent African American.

The principal way city government has an impact on vacancy rates is through the certifiable tax delinquent status provisions. Not all vacant units are certifiable tax delinquent and not all tax delinquent properties are vacant but there is substantial overlap. The 2001 Housing Market Study and Development Strategy report found the following obstacles to the development of vacant units: property assembly costs for developers and non-profits are too high, title problems with lots, soil/environmental costs associated with addressing demolished units buried on the property prior to 1980, and unknown underground infrastructure conditions.

RACIAL AND CLASS SEGREGATION IN HOUSING

In the academic literature on racial segregation in housing, a number of measures have been identified to represent levels of segregation on a citywide level. Most researchers rely upon the dissimilarity measure as a means of comparison. It gives the percentage of all African-Americans who would have to move to achieve an even, or integrated, residential

configuration – one where each census tract replicates the racial composition of the metropolitan area as a whole. According to the 2000 US Census, the total population of the City of Fort Wayne was 205,727. The African-American population numbered 35,752 (or 17.4 percent). If Fort Wayne was an integrated community or race was not a relevant factor in determining occupancy or homeownership location, each census tract would replicate this 17.4 percent figure. According to the Lewis Mumford Center at SUNY-Albany, Fort Wayne ranks 24th in the nation with a dissimilarity score of 70.9. This means that approximately 71 of every 100 African-Americans would have to move from their present location to a white-dominant tract to achieve integration. Fort Wayne ranks behind only Gary in the state of Indiana (which has been for the past 20 years the most segregated city in the United States and in 2000 was ranked second in the nation with a dissimilarity score of 84.1). Fort Wayne ranks ahead of Indianapolis, which was 27th on the list of major metropolitan cities, with a score of 70.7. Rather than the indices decreasing over time, sociologists find that scores have remained remarkably consistent over the past 60 years. Also contrary to perception, segregation indices are highest in the North and Midwest and lowest in the South.

Overall segregation levels have been the highest in the entire history of the nation from the post World War II period to today. Map IV graphically demonstrates the isolation of African-Americans to almost exclusively the

Southeast area of Fort Wayne. Neighborhoods with concentrations of African-Americans at a rate of more than 50 percent are located east of downtown and in the area bordered by Harrison Street on the west, Tillman Road on the south, Wayne Trace on the east, and Lewis Street on the north. The surrounding areas to the east, south, and southwest are 20 to 50 percent African-American. This high concentration is not replicated to the same degree by any other minority group in Fort Wayne.

What is of particular concern is that the tracts with the highest concentrations of African-Americans also have the highest rates of rental occupancy and vacancies. Closely related to the levels of segregation, one finds a concentration of rental occupied housing units in low-income, predominately minority neighborhoods. For example, the correlation between the percent of blacks within specific census tracts of Fort Wayne is positively and strongly associated with percent of rental occupied housing units (r=.446).

The Latino population in Fort Wayne (5.8 percent of the population) had a 2000 dissimilarity score of 45.7. When the Latino population distribution is represented in map form, one finds that the Latino population tends to predominate in three census blocks south of downtown and bordered on the east by Hanna Street, on the south by Rudisill Boulevard, and the west by Harrison and Broadway Streets (see

Map V). The Latino population increased in the entire Fort Wayne Metropolitan area (including the counties of Adams, Allen, DeKalb, Huntington, Wells, and Whitley), from 1990 to 2000, at a rate of 119 percent. The vast majority of those individuals settled in Fort Wayne (71 percent or 11,884). One finds more geographic dispersion than the African-American community but high concentrations still persist and dissimilarity measures have increased from 34.3 in 1990 to 45.7 in 2000. Another form of segregation is the prevalence socioeconomic stratification in housing. Very rarely do we find mixed-income neighborhoods; and as a result, the impacts can be as potentially severe as racial segregation. Map VI details the results from the 1990 US Census using the 2000 Fort Wayne City limits. The median family income of each census tract was grouped according to five categories. The median family income of $50,000 and above is mainly located around the outer limits of the city. It is extremely evident

in the southwest part of the city. Map VII shows that the true measure of economic inequality and its clustering can only be considered at the county level — just beyond the city limits — where median incomes tend to cluster over $80,000 in the Southwestern and Northern suburbs near Aboite and Dupont Road.

The median family income of $20,000 – $29,000 is mainly located in the central area of the city or just outside of the central area in the northern and southern parts of the inner city. The median family income of $20,000 and lower is mainly in the central area of the city. There are only a couple small areas located outside the center of the city.

The overall trends can be seen most clearly in MapVIII. The map shows the geographic concentration of the percentage of persons below poverty in Fort Wayne. There are 11 tracts in the city of Fort Wayne that have above 20% of the people in it below poverty. These tracts are all located directly in the central and southeast sections

of Fort Wayne. Not coincidentally, they also house the majority of the African American and Latino population. These tracts are 11, 12, 13, 14, 16, 17, 18, 19, 20, 27, and 28.97.

For the purposes of potential policy remedies, the identification of low-moderate income census blocks is important due to the numerous state and federal funds available for neighborhood improvement plans and projects. Map IX identifies the 1990 Census tracts that qualified as low to moderate income neighborhoods. A very large portion of the city from Coliseum Boulevard on the east to Ardmore Avenue on the west, State Boulevard on the north, and Tillman Road on the south encompass the majority of low-mod census block groups but additional groups are found in the north and northeast as well as the southwest. Yet, the central city and its surrounding area contain the majority of low-mid income neighborhoods.

Greatest Increases in Disparity Between Minority and White Rejections from the 2002 Acorn Study

The ten MSAs in which the disparity between denial rates for African-American and White applicants increased the most from 2000 to 2001 were: Ft. Wayne, IN (79% increase); Waterbury, CT (72.3%); Kansas City, MO (46.7%); Memphis, TN (39.7%); Milwaukee, WI (38.5%); Jacksonville, FL (32.7%); Little Rock, AR (30.7%); Ft. Worth-Arlington, TX (30.3%); Orange County, CA (30.1%); and Portland, OR (29.4%). The ten MSAs in which the disparity between Latino and white denial rates increased the most from 2000 to 2001 were: Wilmington, DE (63.9% increase); Ft. Wayne, IN (59.2%);

Memphis, TN (55.9%); Las Cruces, NM (45.4%); Columbus, OH (41.5%); Jacksonville, FL (27.7%); Detroit, MI (27.5%); Cleveland, OH (25.4%); St. Louis, MO (24.2%); and Pittsburgh, PA (23.0%).

INCREASES IN MINORITY DENIAL RATES

The African-American denial rate increased from 2000 to 2001 in only eight of the cities included in this report: Ft. Wayne, IN (36.7% increase); Kansas City, MO (23.1%); Waterbury, CT (19.3%); Milwaukee, WI (15.1%); Houma, LA (7.3%); Ft. Worth-Arlington, TX (6.6%);

Pittsburgh, PA (1.7%); and Orange County, CA (0.9%).

The Latino denial rate for conventional loans increased from 2000 to 2001 in only 6 of the cities considered in this study: Ft. Wayne, IN (22.4% increase); Wilmington, DE (18.6%); Memphis, TN (7.0%); Columbus, OH (6.3%); Stamford-Norwalk, CT (4.9%); and Brockton, MA (2.1%).

CONCLUSION

As bleak as the prognosis sounds for the current state of housing in Black Fort Wayne, there are signs of hope and a potential for a positive turn around. There is no question that housing segregation is the most important dilemma facing the city and its citizenry. With the Latino population increasingly finding itself more segregated and separated from White Fort Wayne, the trend that has made Black/White Fort Wayne the 24th most segregated city in the United States seems quite daunting to face. But we only need to look to our public education system to show how legislation and its enforcement can begin to tackle this problem. [The 1980's legal order to degesegrate Fort Wayne Community Schools is a prime example of the impact of enforcement and a commitment to integration.] Recalling that the residential segregation index for Fort Wayne is 70.9, it is interesting to note that in terms of educational

Table 1. Largest Increases in African-American Rejection Ratio For Conventional Home Purchase Mortgages from 2000 to 2001

MSA	2000 Ratio	2001 Ratio	Ratio Change
Ft. Wayne	1.38	2.47	79.0%
Waterbury	1.66	2.86	72.3%
Kansas City	2.29	3.36	46.7%
Memphis	2.47	3.45	39.7%
Milwaukee	4.05	5.61	38.5%
Jacksonville	1.53	2.03	32.7%
Little Rock	1.63	2.13	30.7%
Ft. Worth-Arlington	1.65	2.15	30.3%
Orange County	1.66	2.16	30.1%
Portland	1.84	2.38	29.4%

Source: Acorn Study, 2002

Table 2. Largest Increases in Latino Rejection Ratio For Conventional Home Purchase Mortgages from 2000 to 2001

MSA	2000 Ratio	2001 Ratio	Change in Ratio
Wilmington	1.08	1.77	63.9%
Ft. Wayne	1.25	1.99	59.2%
Memphis	1.88	2.93	55.9%
Las Cruces	1.96	2.85	45.4%
Columbus	1.47	2.08	41.5%
Jacksonville	1.12	1.43	27.7%
Detroit	1.49	1.90	27.5%
Cleveland	1.93	2.42	25.4%
St. Louis	1.61	2.00	24.2%
Pittsburgh	1.39	1.71	23.0%

Source: Acorn Study, 2002

Table 3. Increases in African-American Denial Rates for Conventional Loans from 2000 to 2001

MSA	2000 Denial Rate	2001 Denial Rate	Increase
Ft. Wayne	30.9%	42.3%	36.7%
Kansas City	27.0%	33.3%	23.1%
Waterbury	19.7%	23.5%	19.3%
Milwaukee	27.8%	32.0%	15.1%
Houma	56.7%	60.1%	7.3%
Ft. Worth-Arlington	37.8%	40.3%	6.6%
Pittsburgh	27.9%	28.4%	1.7%
Orange County	23.4%	23.6%	0.9%

Source: Acorn Study, 2002.

segregation, the dissimilarity index (the percent of students who would have to leave their same race school to attend a different race school) for Fort Wayne Community Schools is 20.4 (down from 34.2 in 1990). The overall dissimilarity index for the Fort Wayne metro area is 65.6, which makes it the 80th most segregated school system in the nation. This rate is not significantly lower since it was only FWCS that were forced to desegregate, not the entire Fort Wayne metropolitan area. Segregation can be challenged and remedied; and given the fact that residential segregation is so closely related to high vacancy, high rental, low property value, and high multi-family unit rates, it is of the utmost importance to address this issue head on.

The greatest asset for the betterment of the quality of life of all Fort Wayne residents is its affordability of housing stock. Homeownership needs to become a priority for all interested residents and all real estate parties, both public and private, need to stress the importance of homeownership regardless of race, color, national origin, religion, sex, familial status, and disability. The economic situation will most likely ultimately determine the fate of Black Fort Wayne but there is no question that how we live, who are neighbors are, and our sense of community and belonging ultimately rests on the access to quality housing options.

Table 4. Increases in Latino Denial Rates for Conventional Loans

MSA	2000 Denial Rate	2001 Denial Rate	Increase
Ft. Wayne	27.86%	34.09%	22.4%
Wilmington	14.14%	16.77%	18.6%
Memphis	28.78%	30.80%	7.0%
Columbus	25.87%	27.50%	6.3%
Stamford-Norwalk	22.84%	23.95%	4.9%
Brockton	19.09%	19.49%	2.1%

Source: Acorn Study, 2002.

Map I

Housing

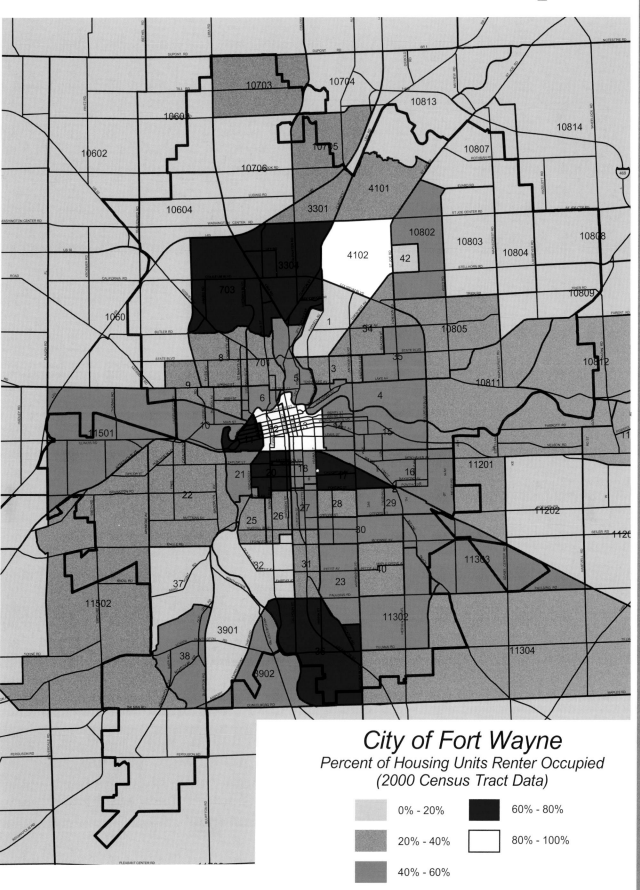

City of Fort Wayne
Percent of Housing Units Renter Occupied
(2000 Census Tract Data)

☐ 0% - 20%	■ 60% - 80%
▨ 20% - 40%	☐ 80% - 100%
▨ 40% - 60%	

Averages: Fort Wayne 38.42%   Allen County 29.00%   Indiana 28.60%

Map II

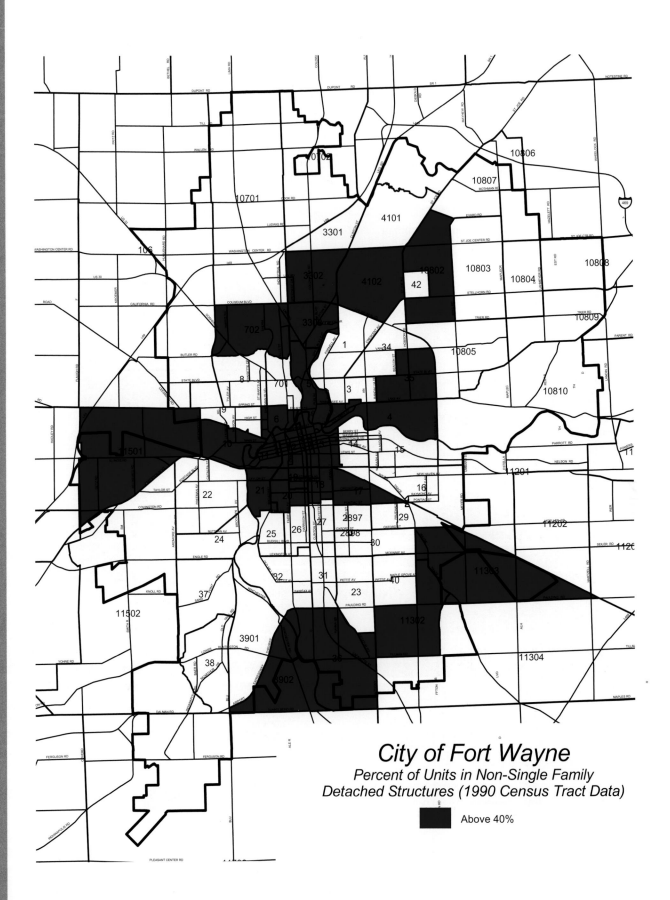

City of Fort Wayne
Percent of Units in Non-Single Family
Detached Structures (1990 Census Tract Data)

Above 40%

The State of Black Fort Wayne • 2003

Map III

Housing

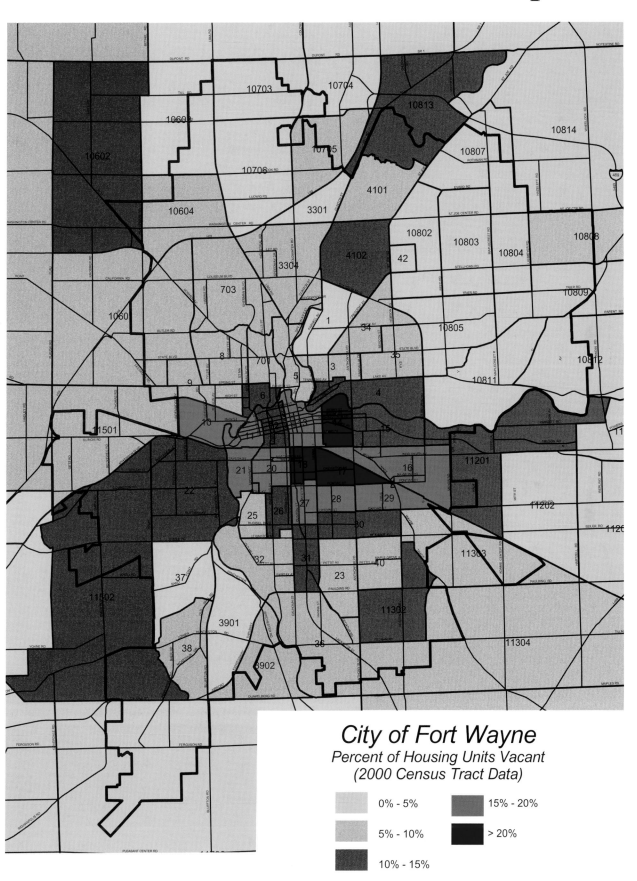

City of Fort Wayne
Percent of Housing Units Vacant
(2000 Census Tract Data)

0% - 5%	15% - 20%
5% - 10%	> 20%
10% - 15%	

Averages: Fort Wayne 8.34%   Allen County 7.31%   Indiana 7.7%

Map IV

City of Fort Wayne
2000 African American Population

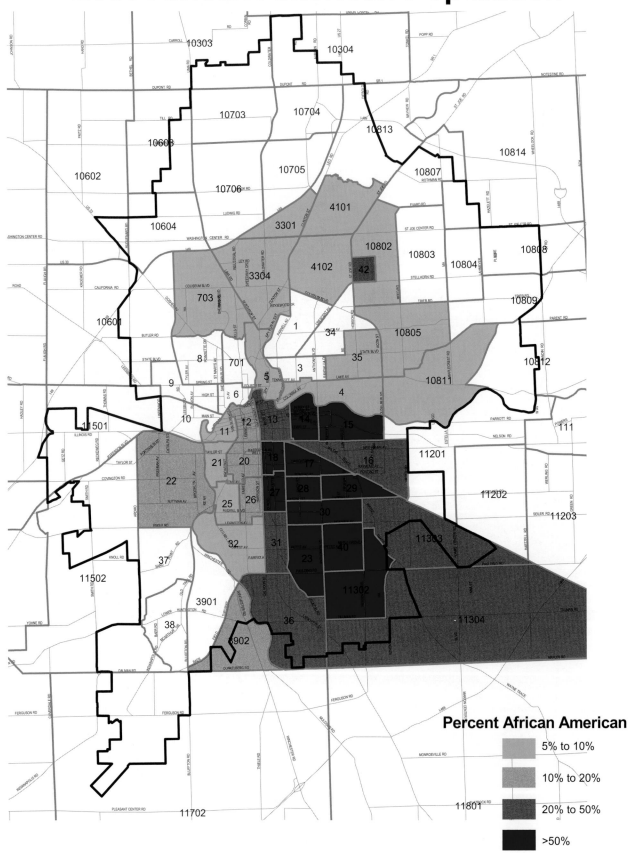

Percent African American

- 5% to 10%
- 10% to 20%
- 20% to 50%
- >50%

Map V

Housing

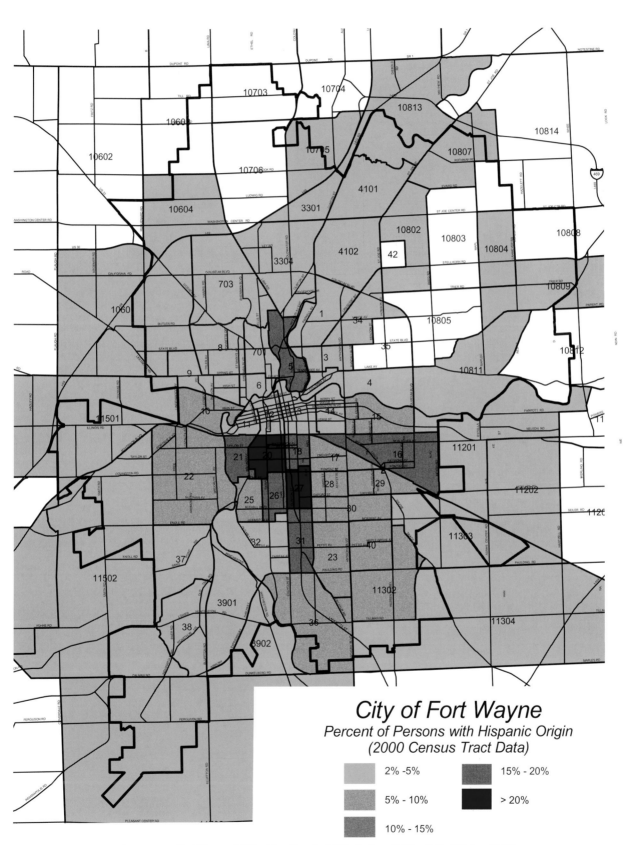

City of Fort Wayne
Percent of Persons with Hispanic Origin
(2000 Census Tract Data)

2% -5%   15% - 20%

5% - 10%   > 20%

10% - 15%

Averages: Fort Wayne 5.8%   Allen County 4.2%   Indiana 3.5%   United States 12.5%

Map VI

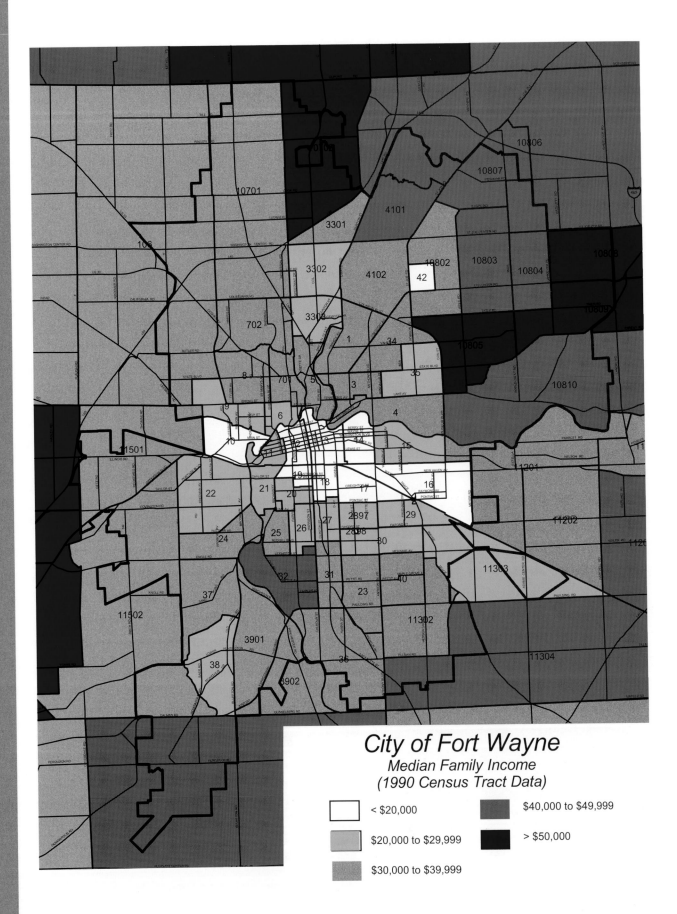

City of Fort Wayne
Median Family Income
(1990 Census Tract Data)

☐ < $20,000	▓ $40,000 to $49,999
▒ $20,000 to $29,999	■ > $50,000
▓ $30,000 to $39,999	

Map VII

Housing

Median Household Income

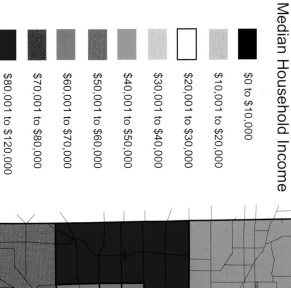

- $0 to $10,000
- $10,001 to $20,000
- $20,001 to $30,000
- $30,001 to $40,000
- $40,001 to $50,000
- $50,001 to $60,000
- $60,001 to $70,000
- $70,001 to $80,000
- $80,001 to $120,000

City of Fort Wayne

Median Household Income by 2000 Census Tracts

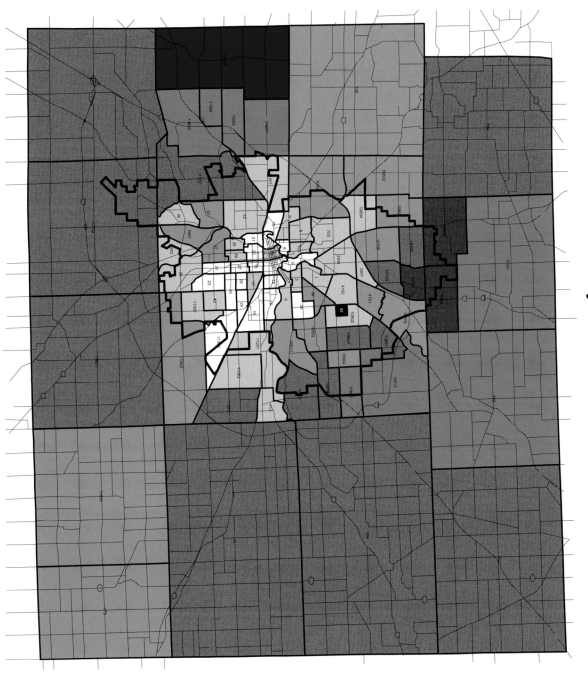

Map VIII

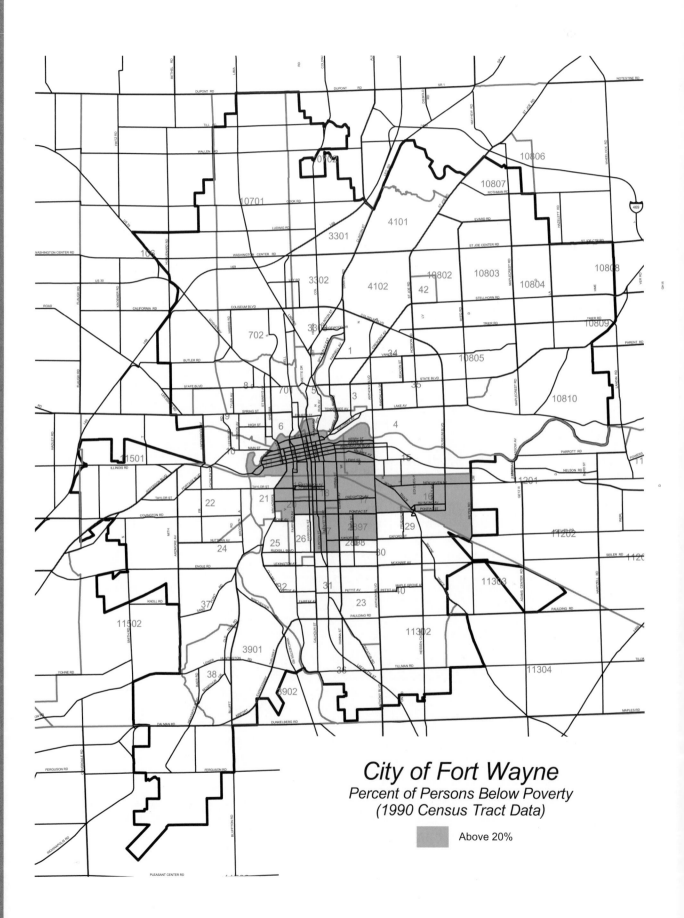

City of Fort Wayne
Percent of Persons Below Poverty
(1990 Census Tract Data)

Above 20%

Map IX

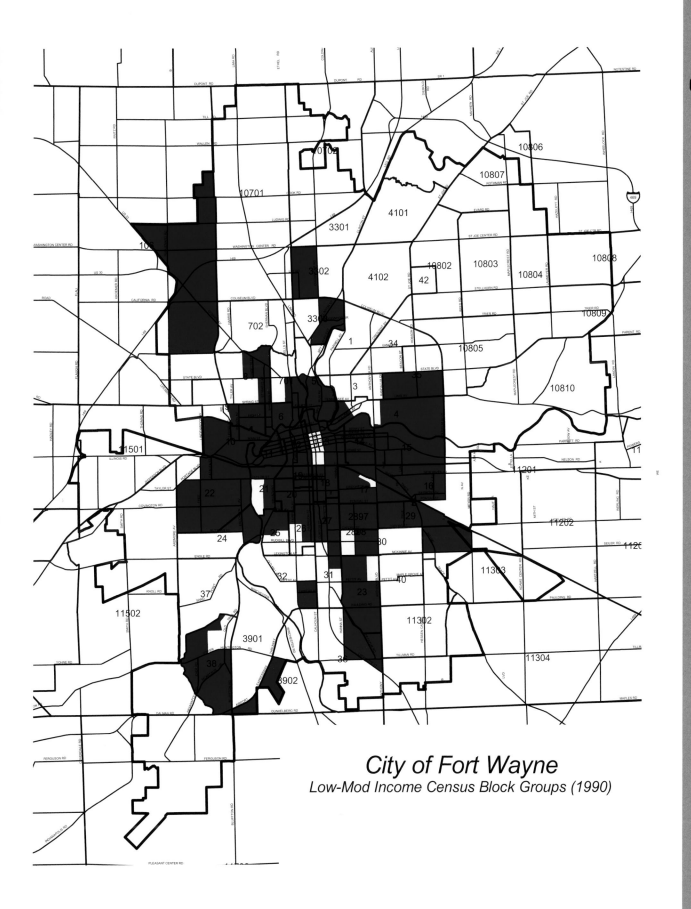

City of Fort Wayne
Low-Mod Income Census Block Groups (1990)

Chapter 3: Employment

Andy J. Barrett • Shayne Abrahams • John Cuellar

INTRODUCTION

The essential ingredient needed to participate in the American Dream is the ability to secure a job that pays a livable wage. The most common measure of the failure for a group of people to achieve this goal is the rate of unemployment for the group. If the rate of unemployment is generally higher for a specific group then additional investigation needs to be done to better understand the effects of the unemployment rate.

The 2000 Census reported an overall unemployment rate of 6.2% for the

only way in which career barriers affect Fort Wayne's African Americans in their effort to attain the American Dream. This chapter will explore what is a livable wage in Indiana and describe the Fort Wayne employment scene for African Americans.

PATHWAYS TO A LIVABLE WAGE

Indiana defines a livable or self-sufficient wage as one "meeting the basic needs in the regular 'marketplace' without public subsidies – such as public housing, food stamps, Medicaid or child

KEY FINDINGS

- The unemployment rate for Fort Wayne's African-American residents is 13.4% compared to white residents, which is 4.5%.

- The unemployment rate for African-American males is three times higher than for white males in the city of Fort Wayne.

- Underemployment among Fort Wayne's African-Americans is extremely high in the Southeast Quadrant.

- Employers in the Southeast Quadrant provide less than 15% of Allen County jobs and wage rates are low compared to the rest of the city.

- Interventions to remedy the causes of the lack of adequate career opportunities have to be identified and undertaken to change the employment prospects for African-American residents.

Table 1 - Labor Force and Unemployment Rates for Fort Wayne in 2000

	Total	White (Non Hispanic)	Black	Minority (Non Black)
Total:				
In Labor Force	107,372	82,506	15,760	9,104
Unemployed	6,642	3,752	2,113	777
Percent Unemployed	6.2%	4.6%	13.4%	8.5%
Male:				
In Labor Force	56,296	43,322	7,456	5,518
Unemployed	3,467	1,977	1,105	385
Percent Unemployed	6.2%	4.6%	14.8%	6.8%
Female:				
In Labor Force:	51,076	39,186	8,304	3,586
Unemployed	3,175	1,775	1,008	392
Percent Unemployed	6.2%	4.5%	12.1%	10.9%

(Source: Census 2000)

City of Fort Wayne and 4.5% for Whites. The historically higher unemployment rate for Blacks is reflected in the 13.4% reported for 2000. Even more disturbing is the more than three times higher unemployment rate for Black males (14.8%) compared to that for White males (4.6%).

This disparity in unemployment rates is a significant barrier for Blacks in the effort to attain a livable wage. However, unemployment is not the

care – or private/informal subsidies – such as free babysitting by a relative or friend, food provided by churches or local food banks, or housing shared with relatives or friends." (Schrock, 1998, p. 1) In 1998, a livable wage occupation was defined as one that provided a minimum annual salary of $20,000. (Warren, 2001, p. 3) The Indiana Economic Development Council updated this figure in

2000 to $22,000. This is the pay at which an occupation for an individual begins to meet the self-sufficiency standard for a family. This may or may not be an adequate amount as

TABLE 2 - Median Weekly Income of Full-time Workers in the US

	1983	1990	2000
White, both sexes	$ 319	$ 424	$ 591
Men	$ 387	$ 494	$ 669
Women	$ 254	$ 353	$ 500
Black, both sexes	$ 261	$ 329	$ 468
Men	$ 293	$ 361	$ 503
Women	$ 231	$ 308	$ 429

(Source: US Bureau of Labor Statistics)

discussed below, but it provides a starting point for the discussion of how well African/Americans are doing relative to the rest of the Indiana population.

Variations in family size, ages of dependents and the community that is being looked at can greatly influence the sufficiency of employment at the minimum for a comfortable non-subsidized life style. The standard is intended to include enough to meet the basic needs including the basic nutritional needs of a family and housing that is not substandard or overcrowded. The $20,000 annual income is comparable to the Federal Poverty Line for a family with one adult and two children of $13,333 in 1998. Food Stamps standard for this size family was $8,928 in Indiana and fulltime employment at the minimum wage would be $10,703.

The Census 2000 reported that 35.7% of African/American households in the United States had household incomes below $20,000 compared to 21.8% of White households. Also, the Bureau of Labor Statistics reported, as displayed in Table 2, that the median

weekly income for full-time employed African/Americans in the United States was $468 and $591 for full-time employed Whites. It is interesting to note in Table 2 that the median income for Black men and White women is almost identical for the year 2000.

Occupations with a minimum annual salary of $20,000 are varied and many can be achieved without completion of a four-year college degree. They can be found in seven career clusters according to a study by the Indiana Economic Development Council and 22% of the Hoosier workforce are employed in these jobs. The clusters or industries are as follows:

· Building and construction
· Business, management and finance
· Health services
· Manufacturing and processing
· Marketing, sales and promotions
· Mechanical repair and precision crafts
· Transportation.

The Fort Wayne metropolitan area has many opportunities for entry-level jobs in these career clusters. However, a study by Abt Associates, Inc. indicates that former welfare recipients in Indiana regardless of

race typically obtained employment in such industries as gasoline services, help supply services, building cleaning, grocery stores, restaurants, and hotels and motels. The exclusion of the career clusters noted for advancing individuals to a livable wage would indicate that the Welfare to Work effort has not placed these individuals on the pathway to a livable wage.

POVERTY RATES FOR AFRICAN AMERICANS IN ALLEN COUNTY

The 2000 census indicates that 22.8% of African American families in Allen County are below the poverty level in income. The rate for all Allen County families is 6.7% and is 4.3% for those classified as White. The percent of African American children under the age of 17 living in poverty is 35.9% compared to 14.8% for all Allen County and 8.4% for White children. In fact, almost as many Black children as White children under the age of 17 live in poverty in Allen County (4680 Black vs. 5439), despite the fact that Allen County has over five times as many White children as Black children. Table 3 provides another view of household incomes in Allen County. Black households are over represented in the lowest income brackets and under represented in the higher ones.

Chart 1 shows a visual representation of Table 3. Household Income appears to be unfavorably distributed at all levels. When it is better to be a higher percentage, the Black households are lower and when it is better to be lower, they are higher, For example, it would be better to have a low percentage of household

Table 3 Incomes in Allen County, Indiana for White and Black Households

	White		Black	
Less than $10,000	6336	5.8%	2464	18.5%
$10,000 to $19,999	12467	11.3%	2156	16.2%
$20,000 to $29,999	14251	12.9%	2417	18.2%
$30,000 to $39,999	14584	13.2%	1659	12.5%
$40,000 to $49,999	13154	11.9%	1274	9.6%
$50,000 to $59,999	11208	10.2%	924	7.0%
$60,000 to $74,999	14066	12.8%	921	6.9%
$75,000 to $99,999	12090	11.0%	757	5.7%
$100,000 and more	11987	10.9%	713	5.4%

(Source: Census 2000 Primary File 3)

Chart 1 - Percent Distribution of Household Income (see Table 3 for statistics - for example Category I level of household income is less than $10,000 and Category 3 is $10,000 to $19,999)

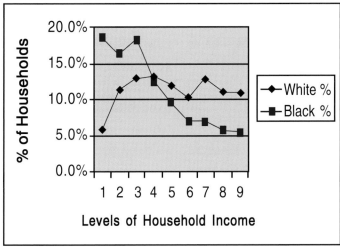

(Source: Census 2000 Summary File 3)

incomes in the less than $10,000 category, but the percentage of Black households in that category is three times higher than the percentage for White households.

UNEMPLOYMENT IN THE SOUTHEAST QUADRANT OF FORT WAYNE

The majority of the data that is available covers Allen County or the City of Fort Wayne. However, there are data that are available by census tract, an area defined by the US Census Bureau as small relatively permanent statistical subdivisions of a county. By combining census data from a number of census tracts in the Southeast quadrant of the City of Fort Wayne, a very telling depiction of the employment picture for African Americans can be obtained.

The data used in this analysis are not made up or adjusted in any fashion. They are combined by simple addition. The statistics in Table 4 summarize the following Fort Wayne Census Tracts: 12-18, 20, 27-31, 36, 40 and 113.02-113.04. The area which is designated as the Southeast

(SE) Quadrant for the purposes of this analysis is generally considered to be bordered on the north by the Maumee River and US. 30 east of downtown, on the east by Adams Center Road, on the south by Tillman and Paulding Roads, and on the west by Calhoun Street and the St. Mary's River.

While the area is populated by approximately 30% of the city's residents, almost 75% of the Blacks in the city reside there. And the average unemployment in 2002 in the selected area in the Southeast Quadrant is over 13.7% compared to 5.3% for all of Fort Wayne and all of Allen County. The percent of Southeast Fort Wayne area's population that is Black is 44.4% while the rest of the City of Fort Wayne outside of the SE quadrant is 6.6%. Looking at the picture from an Allen County point of view reveals similar dramatic contrasts. The percentage of Black residents in all of Allen County is 11.3% while the percentage of Black residents in Allen County not including the city of Fort Wayne is less than 2%. The Southeast

Quadrant can be described as a concentration of African Americans living in poverty and largely unemployed.

UNDEREMPLOYMENT

Underemployment, the inadequacy of employment to the point of a hardship in meeting basic needs of living, is a well documented occurrence among African-Americans. While underemployment is challenging to measure accurately , there is evidence in Fort Wayne provided by the levels of "involuntary part-time work, working poverty, the misfit between educational credentials and employment opportunities, and discouragement" (Johnson, 1995, p. 1). The statistics related to poverty and low household incomes presented earlier in this chapter support the conclusion that substantial underemployment exists in Fort Wayne among the Black population.

The existence of a high rate of underemployment worsens the economic situation in the City and provides another dimension to the social and economic problems faced by the African American residents. However, a different set of solutions targeted at underemployment may be needed rather than those presently being used to address unemployment. Jobs in the Southeast Quadrant.

The number of employment opportunities in the Southeast Quadrant identified above is also disproportionately low. Employers located in the Southeast Quadrant provide less than 15% of the Allen County jobs and the wage rates are relatively low (US Census Bureau Zip Code Business Patterns – 2000). This lack of nearby employment opportunities identifies an additional barrier to employment for a large proportion of the city's Black population – the need for adequate transportation. Employers reasonably expect timely attendance and the lack of a reliable transportation will significantly impair good job performance. There are a number of other barriers to sustainable employment opportunities such as access to education and training.

CONCLUSION AND RECOMMENDATIONS

The employment picture for African American residents of the City of Fort Wayne, particularly those residing in the Southeast Quadrant of the city, is dismal. With high unemployment and extensive underemployment, the key to attainment of the American Dream is very elusive for this generation and generations to come. Poverty, and its associated ills, are and will continue to be a way of life. Interventions to remedy the causes of the lack of adequate career opportunities have to be identified and undertaken to change the prospects for African American residents.

The Realities of Intentional Job Discrimination in Metropolitan America • 1999

INTENTIONAL DISCRIMINATION

Another barrier to adequate employment for African-Americans and other minorities in Fort Wayne is intentional discrimination. The information that follows is from a four year study conducted by Rutgers Law School professors Alfred W. and Ruth G. Blumrosen, The Realities of Intentional Job Discrimination in Metropolitan America—1999. The study, funded by Ford Foundation, was based on employers' annual reports to the federal government from 160,000 establishments employing 37 million workers. "The study found that intentional job discrimination continues on a major scale. Blacks, Hispanics, Asian Pacific workers and White Women who have the knowledge, skills, abilities, and experience to compete are deprived of that opportunity by intentional discrimination between a quarter and a third of the time they seek such opportunities." (I 1999 IJDMA p. 56) A segment of Part III of the study was published separately as Indiana 1999 Intentional Job Discrimination in Metropolitan Areas, by Alfred W. and Ruth G. Blumrosen.

"The Supreme Court held in 1977 that a 'pattern or practice' of intentional job discrimination exists when an employer treats some people less favorably than others as a 'standard operating procedure-the regular rather than the unusual practice.' When there is statistical evidence that an establishment is employing minorities or women in such small numbers that the pattern is unlikely to have occurred by chance, the law presumes that the discrimination is intentional." (I 1999 IJDMA p. 18

"Intentional job discrimination was identified by examining establishment reports in each metropolitan area by industry. Within each industry, nine occupational categories were examined separately. In this way, the average utilization of men and women, Blacks, Hispanics and Asians in each industry and occupational category within each metropolitan area was obtained. Establishments that were so far below the average utilization of minorities or women that it was unlikely to have occurred by chance, stood out 'like sore thumbs' in this analysis....

"Workers affected by this discrimination were measured by the difference between the number actually employed and number that the apparent discriminator would have employed if it had employed minorities/women at the average....The average is not a quota—it is a fact, showing how similar employers have employed minorities and women in the same occupation under the same labor market and industrial circumstance....

KEY FINDINGS

- Despite the initial focus of the Civil Rights Act on Black workers, and the improvement that has taken place since, Black workers still bear the severest brunt of intentional discrimination.

- Every time a Black worker in the Fort Wayne MSA sought an employment opportunity in 1999, he or she had a 43.77% chance of facing discrimination.

- The study concludes that intentional discrimination is still so pervasive that affirmative action programs continue to be necessary.

- The study found that intentional job discrimination continues on a major scale. Blacks, Hispanics, Asian Pacific workers, and White women who have the knowledge, skills, abilities, and experience to compete are deprived of that opportunity by intentional discrimination between a quarter and a third of the time they seek such opportunities.

"The study addresses some of the most common employer explanations for such low levels of minority and female employment, such as women aren't interested in the work,[they are doing the same work for other similar employers]; no qualified workers were available, [qualified workers were available because they were doing the same type of work for other employers.]" (I 1999 IJDMA p. 57) The findings in the main Metropolitan Statistical Areas (MSAs) in Indiana are displayed in Table 4.

severest brunt of this discrimination. They constitute less than half of all minority workers reported, but they were 57% of all workers affected by discrimination. Fifteen percent of all Black workers were so affected in 1999, while 11% of both Hispanics and Asian Pacific workers were affected." (I 1999 IJDMA p.58)

Table 4. Geographic Distribution of Discrimination in the Main MSAs in Indiana, 1999

Affected Workers* in EEO-1 Labor Force in the Largest Metro Statistical Areas - Indiana									
* "Affected Workers" are the difference between the number of members of an affected group employed in an establishment & the number of such workers who would have been employed if the employer had employed that group at the average.									
** White Women as % of All Women: 82.88 %; They are reported here. Minority Women are reported in each minority group.									
Group	Indianapolis MSA		Ft. Wayne MSA		Gary MSA		These 3 MSAs		State Totals
	Affected Workers		Affected Workers		Affected Workers		Affected Workers		
	#	% of Group	#	% of Group	#	% of Group	#	% of Group	#
W. Women**	5,014	55%	1,350	15%	613	7%	6,977	76%	9,315
Blacks	6,951	56%	1,091	9%	2,254	18%	10,296	82%	12,490
Hispanics	1,200	35%	331	10%	1,119	33%	2,651	77%	3,439
Asian-Pac	43	23%	51	27%	0	0%	94	50%	189
Total	13,209	52%	2,823	11%	3,987	16%	20,018	79%	25,253

Source: Indiana 1999 Intentional Job Discrimination in Metropolitan Areas, Alfred W. and Ruth G. Blumrosen, p. 13)

The findings in the Fort Wayne MSA by industry are displayed in Tables 5, 6, and 7. They include data from private sector establishments with 50 or more employees who filed EEO-1 reports. These tables include discrimination by occupational category and by industries for which the authors had sufficient data. "The industries are identified by the Standard Industrial Classification

These three MSAs account for 79% of all affected workers in this state. Included in these MSAs are:

- 76 % of the affected White Women workers.
- 82% of the affected Black workers.
- 77% of the affected Hispanic workers.
- 50 % of the affected Asian-Pacific Origin workers.

The Fort Wayne MSA had 2,823 affected workers (workers who would have been employed if the employer had employed that group at the average). Of these, 1,350 were White Women, 1,091 were Blacks, 331 were Hispanics and 51 were of Asian-Pacific Origin.

Nationwide, the study found that "Despite the initial focus of the Civil Rights Act on Black workers, and the improvement that has taken place since, Black workers still bear the

Table 5. Discrimination Against Blacks by MSA and Industry in Fort Wayne, Indiana, 1999

DISCRIMINATION AGAINST BLACKS	*Comparisons w/Discrimination		Affected Workers	**Discriminating Establishments	
Industry	#	%	#	#	%
Motor Vehicles & Equip.	10	62.50%	227	10	62.50%
Nurs. & Personal Care Facilities	11	47.83%	223	11	50.00
Eating & Drinking Places	22	50.00%	112	22	50.00%
Grocery Stores	17	53.13%	101	16	59.26%
Department Stores	8	30.77%	67	8	34.78%
Hospitals	6	42.86%	66	3	50.00%
Misc. Fabricated Metal Prods.	5	50.00%	39	4	44.44%
Telephone Communication	6	40.00%	35	5	55.56%
Railroads	2	20.00%	5	1	25.00%
SICs with <10 comparisons	29	38.67%	217	27	39.13%
Total	116	43.77%	1,091	107	46.72%

*The percentage of discrimination found under the heading **"Comparisons With Discrimination, %"** (in bold face) represents the probability that a person with the listed race, sex or ethnic characteristics will face intentional discrimination when seeking an employment opportunity in that industry and MSA in any occupation"... Source: Indiana 1999 Intentional Job Discrimination in Metropolitan Areas, Alfred W. and Ruth G. Blumrosen, p. 30.)

"The **Discriminating Establishments section of the table includes the number of establishments that appear to discriminate. It also contains the percentage that that number is of all reporting establishments in that industry and MSA. The percentage probability of discrimination may be smaller than the percentage of discriminating establishments because each discriminating establishment is counted once, regardless of the number of comparisons in that establishment showing discrimination."... Source: Indiana 1999 Intentional Job Discrimination in Metropolitan Areas, Alfred W. and Ruth G. Blumrosen, p. 30-31.)

Source: Indiana 1999 Intentional Job Discrimination in Metropolitan Areas, Alfred W. and Ruth G. Blumrosen, p. 41

System, 1987 (SIC)."...All establishments that had 20 or more employees in that industry and occupation were compared to the mean for their group. (I 1999 IJDMA p. 16)

"Each industry has a possibility of discriminating in each of the occupations for which it has sufficient employees for a comparison. The average, which is the benchmark against which each establishment is measured, is the average employment in the industry of each group of minorities and women for each occupational category. The percentage of discriminating establishments may exceed 50% of all the reporting establishments....

"Discrimination is defined as 1.65 standard deviations or more below the average utilization in the same MSA, SIC and Occupational Category. **Comparisons** are between establishments in the same MSA and SIC and Occupational Category. **Affected Workers** represents the difference between the actual utilization by a discriminating establishment that is at least two standard deviations below the average and the utilization that would exist if the discriminating establishment employed at the average in the same MSA, SIC and occupational category." (I 1999 IJDMA p. 30.)

As shown in Tables 5, 6 and 7, every time a Black worker in the Fort Wayne MSA sought an employment opportunity in 1999, he or she had a 43.77% chance of facing discrimination – almost one-half of

Table 6. Discrimination Against Hispanics by MSA and Industry in Fort Wayne, Indiana, 1999

DISCRIMINATION AGAINST HISPANICS	*Comparisons w/Discrimination		Affected Workers	**Discriminating Establishments	
Industry	#	%	#	#	%
Eating & Drinking Places	23	52.27%	111	23	52.27%
Misc. Plastics Products	5	35.71%	44	5	45.45%
SICs with <10 comparisons	18	54.55%	176	18	56.25%
Total	46	50.55%	331	46	52.87%

* and **, see notes under Table 5.

Source: Indiana 1999 Intentional Job Discrimination in Metropolitan Areas, Alfred W. and Ruth G. Blumrosen, p. 45

the time. A Hispanic worker faced this risk 50.55% of the time, while Asian workers faced it 69.23% of the time.

Almost one-half (107) of the establishments in the Fort Wayne MSA included in this study discriminated against Blacks, affecting 1,091 workers.

More than one-half (46) of the establishments in the Fort Wayne MSA included in this study discriminated against Hispanics, affecting 331 workers.

Almost 70% (9) of the establishments in the Fort Wayne MSA included in this study discriminated against Asians, affecting 51 workers.

CONCLUSION AND RECOMMENDATIONS

(Insert original section from Andy.)

In addition, we must deal with intentional discrimination by employers. "The playing field of employment in this state is clearly not level. The only way this massive problem of intentional discrimination can be usefully and practically addressed is by encouraging establishments to recruit, hire, train, assign, promote, pay and treat qualified minorities and women as they treat qualified Whites and males. This is all that affirmative action programs have ever expected. We know that there are qualified minorities and women in this state, because they are currently working

Table 7. Discrimination Against Asians by MSA and Industry in Fort Wayne, Indiana, 1999

DISCRIMINATION AGAINST ASIANS	*Comparisons w/Discrimination		Affected Workers	**Discriminating Establishments	
Industry	#	%	#	#	%
SICs with <10 comparisons	9	69.23%	51	9	69.23%
Total	9	69.23%	51	9	69.23%

* and **, see notes under Table 5.

Source: Indiana 1999 Intentional Job Discrimination in Metropolitan Areas, Alfred W. and Ruth G. Blumrosen, p. 41

for employers who did not discriminate against them." (I 1999 IJDMA p. 47)

"The study concludes that intentional discrimination is still so pervasive that affirmative action programs continue to be necessary.... Affirmative action programs are intended to allow employers who have reason to be concerned that they might be discriminating to take steps to correct their practices." (I 1999 IJDMA p. 62)

Chapter 4: Poverty and Welfare

Johnathan C. Ray

INTRODUCTION

The chapter begins with an overview of the characteristics of persons receiving three types of welfare assistance in Allen County, Indiana: Temporary Assistance for Needy Families (TANF), Food Stamps and Medicaid. This is followed with historical background on welfare reform. To help put these figures in context, information on the general Whites received TANF assistance, whereas approximately equal numbers of Blacks and Whites received Food Stamps, and far more Whites than Blacks received Medicaid benefits. The TANF program had fewer Black and White recipients than did the Food Stamp and Medicaid programs. The Medicaid program had more Black and White

KEY FINDINGS

- Greatest Number of African-Americans on TANF assistance tend to be within the ages of 6 to 17 years of age.
- The average family exiting the welfare system makes a median annual income of $13,748.
- Welfare reform has found a great deal of domestic violence among welfare-to-work participants.
- African-Americans experience an additional set of variables when overcoming welfare/poverty.
- Some employers are wary of hiring graduates of publicly subsidized programs, believing that something must be wrong with people who are eligible for such efforts.

Figure 1. Number of Clients on TANF, Food Stamps, and Medicaid in Allen County, in May 2002

	TANF Clients	Food Stamp Clients	Medicaid Clients
Black	4,926	10,523	12,971
White	2,941	11,301	19,461

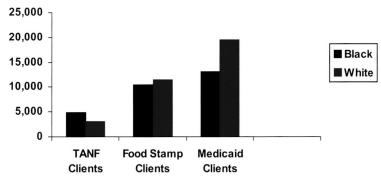

Source: Allen County Division of Family & Children, May 2002

population is presented as well. Next, some of the challenges to effective implementation of welfare reform, including a living wage, the job gap, rural/urban differences, domestic violence, and the role of employers, are discussed. The chapter concludes with suggested approaches to improve welfare reform's success in getting families out of poverty.

The relative <u>numbers</u> of Black and White persons receiving TANF, Food Stamps and Medicaid benefits in Allen County in May, 2002 varied greatly. Substantially more Blacks than

recipients than either of the other two programs. See Figure 1 and Map I. By far the majority of the recipients of TANF benefits were children under 18 years of age. More than 72% of Black TANF recipients and 63% of White TANF recipients in Allen County fell into this category. The persons who received TANF

Figure 2. Number of Individuals Receiving TANF by Race and Age, in Allen County, in May 2002

Race & Age	0-5 yrs	6-17 yrs	18-20 yrs	21-64 yrs	Total
Black	1,642	1,914	182	1,188	4,926
White	900	976	92	973	2,941

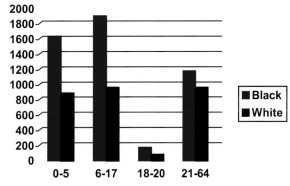

Source: Allen County Division of Family & Children, May 2002

Table 1. Allen County TANF Recipients by Zip Code, May, 2003

Zip Code	Black	White
46802	337	267
46803	1,308	283
46804	43	85
46805	104	287
46806	2,074	372
46807	259	275
46808	67	389
46809	43	131
46814	2	4
46815	148	135
46816	614	105
46818	8	156
46819	46	105
46825	123	242
Sub Total	5,176	2,836

Source: Family and Social Service Administration, May, 2003

Figure 3. Number of Individuals Receiving Food Stamps, By Race and Age, in Allen County, in May, 2002

Race & Age	0-5 yrs	6-17 yrs	18-20 yrs	21-64 yrs	65 +	Total
Black	2,604	3,563	466	3,644	246	10,523
White	2,293	2,923	361	5,208	516	11,301

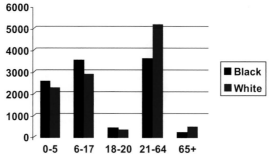

Source: Allen County Division of Family & Children, May 2002

benefits in May 2002 represented approximately 13% of the Black population and 1 % of the White population in Allen County in 1999. See Figure 2 and Table 5.

The largest numbers of Allen County TANF recipients in May, 2003 were clustered within the 46802, 46803, 46806, 46807, and 46816 zip codes, which together accounted for 5,894 or 73.6 % of the total. Black TANF recipients were more highly concentrated than White TANF recipients, with these zip codes housing 4,592 or 88.7% of Black TANF recipients, and 1,302 or 45.9% of White TANF recipients. White TANF recipients were more widely dispersed, with the 46805, 46808, and 46825 zip codes housing a large portion of the White TANF

recipients (918 or 32.4%), but only a few of the Black TANF recipients (294 or 5.7%).

More than 58% of Black Food Stamp recipients and 46% of White Food Stamp recipients in Allen County were children under the age of 18. While the number of Black children was greater than the number of White children on the program, more White adults than Black adults received Food Stamp benefits. The persons who received Food Stamp benefits in May 2002 represented approximately 28% of the Black population and 4 % of the White population in Allen County in 1999. See Figure 3 and Table 5.

The largest numbers of Allen County Food Stamp recipients in May, 2003 were clustered within the 46802, 46803, 46806, 46807, and 46816 zip

codes, which together accounted for 14,897 or 65.8% of the total. Black Food Stamp recipients were more highly concentrated than White Food Stamp recipients, with these zip codes housing 9,903 or 86.8% of Black Food Stamp recipients, and 4,994 or 44.4% of White Food Stamp recipients. White Food Stamp recipients were more widely dispersed, with the 46805, 46808, 46815, 46818 and 46825 zip codes housing a large portion of the White

Table 2. Allen County Food Stamp Recipients by Zip Code, May, 2003

Zip Code	Black	White
46802	694	1,240
46803	2,323	834
46804	122	352
46805	338	1,321
46806	4,757	1,226
46807	638	1,100
46808	165	1,500
46809	117	455
46810	0	1
46813	0	1
46814	2	14
46815	297	563
46816	1,491	594
46818	26	596
46819	107	364
46825	326	1,080
Sub Total	11,403	11,241

Source: Family and Social Service Administration, May, 2003

Table 3. Allen County Medicaid Recipients by Zip Code, May, 2003

Zip Code	Black	White
46802	647	1,313
46803	2,443	896
46804	155	668
46805	468	2,102
46806	5,363	1,445
46807	715	1,445
46808	164	1,985
46809	130	709
46810	0	1
46814	6	72
46815	388	1,173
46816	1,819	973
46818	68	1,080
46819	159	551
46825	370	1,750
Subtotal	12,895	16,167

Source: Family and Social Service Administration, May, 2003

Figure 4. Number of Individuals Receiving Medicaid, by Race and Age, in Allen County, in May, 2002

Race & Age	0-5 yrs	6-17 yrs	18-20 yrs	21-64 yrs	65 +	Total
Black	3,645	5,519	561	2,743	503	12,971
White	5,186	6,495	713	5,161	1,906	19,461

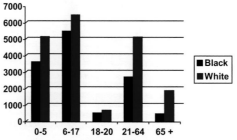

Source: Allen County Division of Family and Children, May 2002

Food Stamp recipients (5,060 or 45.0%), but relatively few of the Black Food Stamp recipients (1,152 or 10.1%).

More than 70% of Black Medicaid recipients and 60% of White Medicaid recipients in Allen County were children under 18 years of age. A greater number of Whites than Blacks in each age group received Medicaid benefits. The persons who received Medicaid benefits in May 2002 represented approximately 34% of the Black population and 7 % of the White population in Allen County in 1999. See Figure 4 and Table 5.

More than one-half of Allen County Medicaid recipients in May, 2003 were clustered within the 46802, 46803, 46806, 46807, and 46816 zip codes, which together accounted for 17,059 or 58.7% of the total. Black Medicaid recipients were more highly concentrated than White Medicaid recipients, with these zip codes housing 10,987 or 85.2 % of Black Medicaid recipients, and 6,072 or 37.6% of White Medicaid recipients. White Medicaid recipients were widely dispersed, with the 46805, 46808, 46815, 46818 and 46825 zip codes also housing a large portion of the White Medicaid recipients (8,089 or 50.0%), but relatively few of the Black Medicaid recipients (1,458 or 11.3%).

WELFARE REFORM

Welfare reform was initiated in Indiana May, 1995, one year prior to the Federal Personal Responsibility and Work Opportunity Reconciliation Act of 1996 (PRWORA). Because a large percentage of welfare recipients have limited work histories and marketable skills, it is hard for them to make a living wage and thus break the cycle of dependence on welfare. Welfare reform was created to help them overcome this disadvantage and move out of poverty.

PRWORA was a reaction to the 1935 Social Security Act, which was established to eliminate poverty. The Social Security Act put in place not just Social Security, but also Unemployment Insurance and Aid to Families with Dependent Children (AFDC). PRWORA changed AFDC's title to Temporary Assistance for Needy Families (TANF) as well as changing AFDC from an entitlement program to a non-entitlement program. Families currently have a lifetime limit of five (5) years and able-bodied adults are limited to two (2) years of TANF assistance.

TANF initiated a change in perspective, moving clients from an entitlement mentality to a work-first attitude. The focus under the old legislation, Aid to Families with

Table 4. Allen County Population Characteristics, 1999

Total Population	331,849
Total Adults In Workforce	173,350
- Adult Population With A High School Diploma	81%
-Adult Population With A B.A. Or Higher Degree	19%.
Total Married Families W/Children	31,048
Total Married Families Without Children	35,203
Total Single Parent Families	12,836
Average Household Income	$44,141
Per Capita Income	$28,985
Poverty Rate In Allen County	7%
Poverty Rate In Indiana.	9%

Source: American Fact Finder, U.S. Census Bureau, 1999.

Table 5. Allen County Population by Race and Poverty Status, 1999

Total Population	331,849
Total White Population	275,697
-% Of Total Population	83%
-# Living In Poverty	15,054
-%Living In Poverty	5.6%
Total African-American Population	37,527
-% Of Total Population	11%
-# Living In Poverty	7,345
-% Living In Poverty	19.6%

Source: American Fact Finder, U.S. Census Bureau, 1999.

Figure 5. Percent of Total Population by Race in Allen County, 1999

White Population: 83%

African-American Population: 11%

Source: American Fact Finder, U.S. Census Bureau, 1999.

Dependent Children, was on assistance to children. The TANF program has its primary focus on the adult being able to provide family support for the children by seeking and maintaining employment.

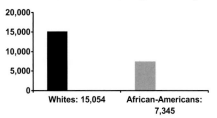

Figure 6. Number of Persons Living in Poverty in Allen County, by Race, 1999

Whites: 15,054   African-Americans: 7,345

Source: American Fact Finder, U.S. Census Bureau, 1999.

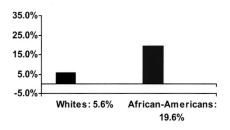

Figure 7. Percent of Racial Group Living in Poverty in Allen County, 1999

Whites: 5.6%   African-Americans: 19.6%

Source: American Fact Finder, U.S. Census Bureau, 1999.

In Fort Wayne, the Allen County Division of Family and Children found that moving people into the labor force may indeed be the best first step in moving them out of poverty. However this, in and of itself, is not likely to achieve the more important workforce development goal of enabling people to keep their jobs and leave poverty behind. Finding a job is the first step to becoming self-sufficient. Keeping a job and moving up the employment ladder via pay and/or promotion is more difficult. The latter is particularly true for people without much employment experience, including many African-Americans, whose unemployment

rate has historically been more than twice the unemployment rate for Whites.

GENERAL POPULATION CHARACTERISTICS

In 1999, the total population in Allen County was 331,849, ranking us third highest state-wide, with 5.5% of the state total.

The workforce in Allen County was comprised of 173,350 adults. Within our adult population, 81% had a high school diploma, and 19% had a B.A. or higher degree.

The total number of married families with children in Allen County was 31,048, as compared to 35,203

married families without children and 12,836 single parent families.

The average household income was $44,141, ranking Allen County eighteenth in the State of Indiana. Our per capita income of $28,985 ranked eighth in the State of Indiana. The poverty rate for Allen County was 7%, while the poverty rate in Indiana was 9%.

Of our total population, Whites comprised 275,697, or 83%, and African-Americans comprised 37,527, or 11%, as shown in Figure 5 and Table 5 below.

In Allen County, 15,054, or 5.6 % of Whites and 7,345 or 19.6% of African-Americans were living in poverty in 1999, as shown in Table 5 and Figures 6 and 7.

A LIVING WAGE AND THE JOB GAP

The Indiana Economic Development Council, Inc., (IEDC) indicated that one key to real welfare reform is establishing just what a living wage is. IEDC defined a livable income "as an income level sufficient to meet the household's basic needs." It is generally accepted that the basic needs of a family include food, shelter, health care, transportation, childcare, and household and personal expenses.

Table 6. Household & Personal Budget, Single Parent Family of Three, Average Age

Food	$377
Housing	$481
Health Care	$206
Child Care	$506
Transportation	$205
Subtotal	$1,775
Household & Personal Expenses @ 10%	$178
Total Monthly Budget	**$1,953**
Annual Budget	*$23,436*
Annual Pre-tax Income Required	*$26,823*

Source: Indiana Economic Development Council, Inc.

Based on the latter definition, welfare and working poor families in our community face a serious problem. Quite simply, many hard-working men and women do not earn enough to make ends meet. IEDC states that a livable wage for a family of three is $24,058-$28,878. The average family exiting the welfare system makes a median annual income of $13,748 (Midwest Partners).

The Indiana economy is in recession. Therefore, the search for jobs is more competitive. Employers can afford to be more selective. Prior to Indiana's recent recession the Midwest Job Gap Project reported that there was a 3-1 job gap in Allen County between low-skilled workers and low-skilled living-wage jobs. These numbers have been exacerbated by the high number of skilled and experienced workers currently seeking employment. The current reality and economic indicators for welfare recipients are less than favorable. In getting and keeping a living wage-job, African-American recipients face not only the same challenges as every other welfare client, but also the significant impact of racial bias, cultural difference, and limited access to transportation.

RURAL/URBAN DIFFERENCES

Welfare reform is distinctly different in rural and urban areas. Dr. William Julius Wilson stated, "The issue is not welfare but the disappearance of work in the ghetto." The problem has now reached catastrophic proportions, and if it isn't addressed it will have lasting and harmful consequences for the quality of life in the cities and, eventually for the lives of all Americans." Dr. Wilson clearly explains in an article that appeared in the New York Times [August 18, 1996/Section 6] that poor communities without work opportunities are different from poor communities where the majority of the able-bodied adult population is employed. Dr. Wilson believes that the relocation of factories and industries from urban to suburban areas has negatively impacted African-Americans, who reside primarily in urban areas. Lack of a work experience negatively affects communities and culture. Dr. Wilson says," Work is not simply a way to make a living and support your family. It also constitutes a framework for daily behavior because it imposes discipline."

Without persistent, strategic and innovative efforts by the government to reinvest in urban communities, welfare reform may be headed toward an unsuccessful outcome. Welfare reform will have to be approached and handled differently by suburban and urban communities.

DOMESTIC VIOLENCE.

Domestic violence is another barrier that keeps some women on welfare. Welfare reform has found a great deal of domestic violence among welfare-to-work participants. The abusive partner in many cases sabotages and prevents low-income women from gaining education and employment. In many instances the violence and abuse does not end when the abused partner ends the relationship. Many time violence and sabotage increase. Some victims of domestic violence "suffer from traumatic effects of the abuse, resulting in symptoms like depression, persistent anxiety, and post-traumatic stress disorder, which seriously affect women's ability to seek and maintain employment [Family Resource Coalition of American Report, Winter, 1998-99, volume17].

EMPLOYERS' ROLE IN WELFARE REFORM

Clearly, engaging employers heavily in welfare reform is a good starting point for reforming the system and eliminating poverty. However, at least two significant barriers exist to meaningful employer involvement.

First, the public and private sectors typically have different workforce

Table 7. Prevalence of Domestic Violence Among Women Receiving Welfare

Study	Currently Experiencing Physical Violence*	Have Experienced Physical Violence Ever as Adults
Passaic County Study of AFDC Recipients in a Welfare-to-Work Program	14.6%	57.3%
In Harm's Way? Domestic Violence, AFDC Recipients, and Welfare Reform in Mass.	19.5%	64.9%
The Worcester Family Research Project	32.5%	60.6%
The Effects of Violence on Women's Employment	31.1%	33.9%

*Definitions of "physical violence" and of "currently" varied from study to study

Source: Family Resource Coalition of America Report - Winter 1998-99 – Vol. 17. No. 4

objectives, making collaboration difficult. Employers want employees who will contribute to productivity and profitability. To the extent that public agencies can help them achieve this goal, employers are willing to participate. To the extent that the private sector is asked to sacrifice productivity and profitability in pursuit of other objectives, employers are understandably less eager to participate. Historically, the public sector has focused on job placement for the disadvantaged, with a strong emphasis on the hardest to serve, such as long-term welfare recipients. As a result, many employers are wary of hiring graduates of publicly subsidized programs, believing that something must be wrong with people who are eligible for such efforts. The latter is compounded further by the introduction of race and race biases. While the private and public sector goals are not mutually exclusive, finding common ground remains difficult.

Second, while some private employers are willing to work with public agencies to address the employment needs of poor people, they believe that public agencies must lead the effort. It has been a mistake for public agencies to assume that private employers are planning to hire welfare clients or other poor people simply because of a social obligation or change in federal law.

CONCLUSION

Welfare as we knew it is dead. The focus of Temporary Assistance for Needy Families is and will remain on able-bodied adults getting and keeping jobs. But compelling arguments can be made that the children are the ultimate intended beneficiaries of reform since improvements in their parents' lives generally are believed to benefit them. In addition to the effect of welfare reform on individual adults and their children, the effect of the reforms on the membership or functioning of the family as a whole is of interest, as is their impact on the community and neighborhoods.

Clearly, our approach to poverty and welfare should take two primary macro-positions. First, we must understand that welfare clients can and do get jobs, but they lose them at a higher rate than the general public because of problems related to being poor single parents, cultural differences or issues, and concerns related to having limited work histories and limited job skills. Second, we must understand that African-Americans experience an additional set of variables when overcoming welfare/poverty. A successful approach to welfare reform must encompass both macro-positions.

Whatever strategies public welfare implements for getting families out of poverty, a clear and concrete understanding of poverty's various dimensions must be our highest priority. There is no quick fix. If welfare-to-work programs are to be successful, the welfare-to-work process must be viewed from a human perspective. If welfare recipients are to develop into steady workers, we have to create a system that reflects what we know about how people learn and grow.

We have to wrestle with some tough questions. Work requirements and time limits alone will not be enough to turn a large and diverse welfare population into steady workers. If this is to happen, we will have to begin to think differently about the nature of welfare recipients and the system. Reforming the system requires a change in the community's willingness to work together creating a win-win situation for everyone no matter what his or her mission is – purely altruistic or purely personal.

Map I

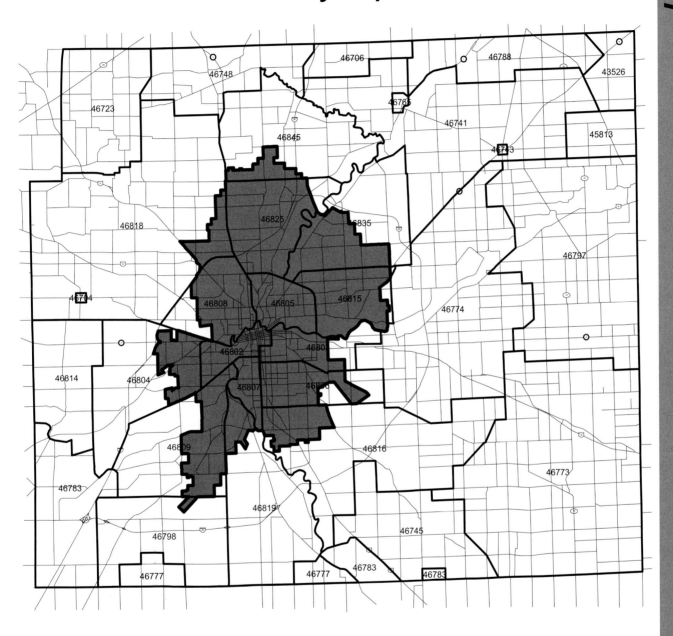

Allen County Zip Codes

Chapter 5: Business & Economic Development

A.V. Fleming, D.B.A.

INTRODUCTION

This chapter will discuss the following aspects of Business and Economic Development as it relates to African-Americans throughout the United States and the city of Fort Wayne: African-Americans total buying power, average annual expenditures by African-Americans, African-American owned businesses, and the survey methodology used to identify African-American businesses.

AFRICAN AMERICAN BUYING POWER

African-American communities around the country affect the United States economy significantly. According to the Selig Center for Economic Growth, Terry College of Business, at the University of Georgia, African-Americans increase in number and purchasing power, and their share of the U.S. consumer market draws more and more attention from producers and retailers alike. African-Americans spent $532.7 billion in 1999 and are projected to spend $682 billion by 2006.) African-Americans share of total U.S. buying power was 8.2%, in 1999, up from 7.4% in 1990, and in

KEY FINDINGS

- African-Americans buying power grew at an annual rate of 6.3% from 1990 to 1999.

- Fort Wayne's African-American residents spent $555 million dollars in 1999.

- Largest group of businesses owned by African-Americans in Fort Wayne tend to be in the service industry.

- African-Americans makeup 27% of all minority and women owned businesses.

- African-Americans Entrepreneur's in Fort Wayne need assistance in small business accounting, management, and financial assistance.

Table 1

Black Share of Total Buying Power for U.S. and Selected States, 1990 and 1999

(percent)

Area	1990	1999	Area	1990	1999
United States	7.4	8.2	Montana	0.2	0.2
Alabama	14.2	15.4	New York	10.6	11.8
California	5.0	5.0	Ohio	6.9	7.8
District of Columbia	41.7	39.1	South Carolina	17.1	18.1
Florida	7.0	8.4	Texas	7.1	7.7
Illinois	8.6	9.3	Virginia	11.3	12.8
Indiana	5.2	5.7	West Virginia	2.2	2.3
Kentucky	4.8	5.1	Wyoming	0.6	0.9
Maryland	17.4	20.4			
Michigan	9.1	9.8			
Mississippi	19.1	20.8			
Montana	0.2	0.2			
New York	10.6	11.8			

Source: The Selig Center for Economic Growth, Terry College of Business, The University of Georgia, 1998.

Table 2

Black Buying Power by Place of Residence for U.S. and Selected States, 1990 and 1995-1999

(millions of dollars)

Area	1990	1995	1996	1997	1998	1999
United States	308,096	422,164	450,130	475,137	501,983	532,667
Alabama	7,824	11,012	11,695	12,189	12,737	13,398
California	27,528	33,441	35,262	36,961	38,839	40,925
District of Columbia	5,485	6,232	6,406	6,562	6,716	6,920
Florida	15,487	23,001	25,041	26,708	28,641	30,686
Illinois	17,376	23,536	25,015	26,309	27,714	29,389
Indiana	4,325	6,078	6,444	6,748	7,078	7,453
Kentucky	2,345	3,169	3,379	3,555	3,745	3,969
Maryland	15,989	21,926	23,463	24,884	26,305	27,939
Michigan	13,733	18,958	19,886	20,726	21,676	22,887
Mississippi	5,719	8,373	9,016	9,376	9,774	10,248
Montana	22	36	39	39	41	42
New York	37,398	48,429	51,388	54,173	57,306	60,906
Ohio	11,859	16,286	17,254	18,083	19,071	20,287
Tennessee	6,960	10,267	10,875	11,451	12,055	12,762
Texas	18,629	26,726	28,647	30,583	32,860	35,273
Utah	114	198	221	241	261	282
Vermont	20	42	48	49	51	53

Source: The Selig Center for Economic Growth, Terry College of Business, The University of Georgia, 1998.

1999 African-Americans accounted for 5.7% of total buying power in Indiana. (See Table 1)

The buying power of Indiana African-Americans has grown over the years. Black consumers in Indiana spent $4.3 billion in 1990, $6.1 billion in 1995, $6.4 billion in 1996, $6.8 billion in 1997, $7.1 billion in 1998, and $7.5 billion in 1999. (See table 2) The African-American population of Indiana in 1999 was 497,976 and Fort Wayne had 36,604 African-Americans or 7.4% of the African-American population in Indiana. (See Table 3.) Based on our estimates Fort Wayne's African-

American residents spent $555 million in 1999.

In 1999 African-Americans in Fort Wayne spent more than the average for all consumers on food at home, shelter, natural gas, electricity, telephone, water and other public services, apparel, transportation, personal care products and services. (See Table 4.)

These data may suggest that the African-American market sector offers opportunity for increased sales in food, transportation, apparel, and services. Table 5 represents the amount spent by African-American consumers in Fort Wayne for 1999.

Table 3

Population Estimates by Race in Indiana and Fort Wayne

Area	Year	Total Indiana Black Population	Total Fort Wayne Black Population	Percent of Total State Population
Indiana and Fort Wayne	1999	497,976	36,604	7.4%

Source: Indiana State Chamber

AFRICAN AMERICAN OWNED BUSINESSES IN THE FORT WAYNE METROPOLITAN STATISTICAL AREA (MSA)

The Fort Wayne MSA is made up of six counties: Adams, Allen, De Kalb, Huntington, Wells, and Whitley. Data in Table 6 are from 1997 as provided by the U.S. Census Bureau.

As Table 6 shows, in 1997 African-Americans owned 570 of the 23,340 firms in Allen County. All Allen County firms had sales and receipts totaling $34,478,611. The 7,216 firms with paid employees had sales and receipts totaling $33,904,523,000. These firms had 176,987 paid employees and their payrolls totaled $4,720,611,000.

Of the 570 Black-owned firms in Allen County, 86 had paid employees ranging from 1,000 to 2,449. In order to reach the sales and receipt figure of $48,846,000 for Black-owned companies we had to extrapolate. This was done by subtracting the sales and receipts from minorities other than African-Americans from the total of all minorities:

All minorities

$183,947,000

Hispanics

-        10,846,000

American Indian and Alaska Natives

-        60,383,000

Asian and Pacific Islanders

-        65,842,000

African-Americans

$48,846,000

In the Fort Wayne MSA, African-Americans operated 572 businesses in eight of the major groups identified by Standard Industrial Classification (SIC) codes. (See Table 7.)

As Table 7 shows, in 1997 the service industry (exc. membership org & private households) accounted for

Table 4

Average Annual Expenditures by Item as a Percent of After-Tax Money Income for Fort Wayne African American Consumers and All Consumers

	Expenditures as a Percent of After-Tax Income	
	African Americans	All Consumers
Item	(percent)	(percent)
Food - At Home	10.1	8.3
Food - Away From Home	4.1	5.0
Alcoholic Beverages	0.6	0.8
Shelter	18.5	17.5
Natural Gas	1.3	0.8
Electricity	3.5	2.6
Fuel Oil and Other Fuels	0.2	0.3
Telephone	3.2	2.1
Water and Other Public Services	0.9	0.8
Household Operations	1.3	1.5
Housekeeping Services	1.0	1.3
Household Furnishings and Equipment	3.5	4.1
Apparel	7.3	5.0
Transportation	18.5	17.8
Health Care	4.4	5.1
Entertainment	3.8	4.8
Personal Care Products and Services	1.5	1.2
Reading	0.3	0.5
Education	1.1	1.4
Tobacco and Smoking Supplies	0.7	0.8
Miscellaneous	1.9	2.3
Cash Contributions	2.3	2.7
Personal Insurance and Pensions	7.6	8.8
House hold income	$21,037	$32,632

Source: The Consumer Expenditure Survey, Division of Consumer Expenditure Surveys, Office of Prices and Living Conditions, Bureau of Labor Statistics 1999.

Table 5

Average Annual Expenditures by Item in Dollars of After-Tax Money Income for Fort Wayne African American

Item	Percent	Dollars Spent
Food - At Home	10.10%	56,055,000
Food - Away From Home	4.10%	22,755,000
Alcoholic Beverages	0.06%	333,000
Shelter	18.50%	102,675,000
Natural Gas	1.30%	7,215,000
Electricity	3.50%	19,425,000
Fuel oil and Other Fuels	0.02%	111,000
Telephone	3.20%	17,760,000
Water and Other Public Services	0.09%	499,500
Household Operations	1.30%	7,215,000
Housekeeping Services	1.00%	5,550,000
Household Furnishings and Equipment	3.50%	19,425,000
Apparel	7.30%	40,515,000
Transportation	18.50%	102,675,000
Health Care	4.40%	24,420,000
Entertainment	3.80%	21,090,000
Personal Care Products and services	1.50%	8,325,000
Reading	0.03%	166,500
Education	1.10%	6,105,000
Tobacco and Smoking Supplies	0.07%	388,500
Miscellaneous	1.90%	10,545,000
Cash Contribution	2.30%	12,765,000
Personal Insurance and Pension	7.60%	42,180,000

Source: The Consumer Expenditure Survey, Division of Consumer Expenditure Surveys, Office of Prices and Living Conditions, Bureau of Labor Statistics 1999.

the Fort Wayne MSA. Their total sales and receipts were $1,604,000 and 9 of the firms had 20 to 99 employees. Transportation, communication, and utilities accounted for 16 firms, 1 of which had 20 to 99 employees. The finance, insurance and real estate industry (excluding subdividing and development) accounted for 10 firms. The wholesale trade industry accounted for 9 firms, with 0-19 employees. Manufacturing accounted for 3 Black-owned firms in the Fort Wayne MSA.

SURVEY METHODOLOGY

According to the U.S. census all firms operating during 1997, except those classified as agricultural, are represented in the surveys cited above. The information was compiled from a combination of business tax returns and data collected on other economic census

Table 6 Minority-and Women-Owned Businesses

Group	All firms		Firms with paid employees			
	Firms (number)	Sales and Receipts ($1,000)	Firms (number)	Sales and Receipts ($1,000)	Employees	Payroll ($1,000)
Universe (All Firms)	23,340	34,478,611	7,216	33,904,523	176,987	4,720,611
Total minorities	1,281	183,947	268	156,648	2,380	50,656
Black	570	D	86	D	1000 to 2499	D
Hispanic	294	10,846	42	D	100 to 249	D
American Indian and Alaska Natives	160	60,383	15	56,766	414	13,652
Asian and Pacific Islander	273	65,842	125	51,974	713	19,216
Women	5,647	848,847	803	790,052	7,062	148,823

D Withheld to avoid disclosure; **N** Not available; **S** Withheld because data do not meet publication standards;
Source: 1997 U.S. Economic Census: Minority- and Women-Owned Business Enterprises

419 firms or 73% of all Black firms in the Fort Wayne MSA. These firms had total sales and receipts of $27,527,000. Of the 419 firms, 60 had sales and receipts totaling $22,829,000, and had 964 employees. The payroll for these firms was $13,767,000. Retail, the next largest group of Black-owned businesses, accounted for 50 firms with a total of

$9,955,000 in sales and receipts. Of these 50 firms, 16 had sales and receipts of $9,267,000 and payrolls totaling $1,227,000. Industries not classified accounted for 36 firms and made up 7% of the Black-owned firms in the Fort Wayne MSA. Construction industries, subdividers, and developers accounted for 32 firms or 6% of the Black owned firms in

reports. The Census Bureau obtains electronic files from the IRS for all companies filing IRS Form 1040, Schedule C (individual proprietorship or self employed person); 1065 (partnership); any one of the 1120 corporation tax forms; or 941 (Employer's Quarterly Federal Tax Return). The IRS provided certain identification, classification, and

Business and Economic Development

Table 7 Major Industry Groups

Black Major Industry Group (SIC based)	All firms		Firms with paid employees			
	Firms (number)	Sales and Receipts ($1,000)	Firms (number)	Sales and Receipts ($1,000)	Employees	Payroll ($1,000)
All industries	572	48,510	87	40,612	1,073	15,744
Construction industries and subdividers and developers	32	1,604	9	D	20 to 99	D
Manufacturing	3	D	0	0	0	0
Transportation, communications, & utilities	16	D	1	D	20 to 99	D
Wholesale trade	9	D	1	D	0 to 19	D
Retail trade	50	9,955	16	9,267	61	1,227
Finance, insurance and real estate industries (ex sub & dev)	10	D	0	0	0	0
Service industries (exc membership org & private households)	419	27,527	60	22,829	964	13,767
Industries not classified	36	D	0	0	0	

Source: 1997 Economic Census: Minority- and Women -Owned Business Enterprises

measurement data for businesses filing those forms. For most firms with paid employees, the Census Bureau also collected employment, payroll, receipts, and kind of business information for each plant, store, or physical location during the 1997 Economic Census.

In designing the sample, the Census Bureau used several sources of information to identify the probability that a business was minority- or women-owned. For all sole proprietorships, partnerships, and corporations that filed electronic tax forms, the SSA provided gender and race codes for the owners. Persons applying for Social Security Numbers (SSNs) prior to 1981 could categorize their race as (a) White, (b) Black, or (c) Other. In 1981, the racial descriptions on social security applications were expanded to (a) Asian, Asian-American, or Pacific Islander, (b) Hispanic, (c) Black, (d) Northern American Indian or Alaskan Native, and (e) White. Most persons who currently own businesses applied for their SSNs prior to 1981. Therefore, the

majority of owners could be classified only as (a) White, (b) Black, or (c) Other by use of SSA race codes. For each owner, the SSA also provided the Census Bureau with the individual's country of birth, current surname, original surname, mother's maiden surname, and father's surname. The Census Bureau has developed lists of American Indian, Asian, and Hispanic surnames based on research using prior survey data. In addition to the SSA data, several other sources were used to pre-identify businesses by race, ethnicity, and gender of owner(s) as potentially minority-owned:

• Lists of minority- and women-owned businesses published in syndicated magazines, located on the Internet, or disseminated by trade or special interest groups.
• Word strings in the company name indicating possible minority ownership (derived from 1992 survey responses).
• Racial distributions for various state-industry classes (derived from 1992 survey responses) and racial distributions for various ZIP Codes. Individual proprietors who reported

they were of minority ancestry in the 1992 survey and were still active in 1997 were excluded from the mail canvass and the 1992 responses were used instead.

SUMMARY

African-American buying power grew at an annual rate of 6.3% from 1990 to 1999, which is faster than the United States Consumer Price Index (CPI) average growth. The U.S. CPI by the year 2006 will increase 28.7%, but Black buying power is projected to grow more than two and one half times as fast as inflation during the same period according to the U.S. Census Bureau. Substantially above-average growth in African-American buying power demonstrates the growing importance of African American consumers and should create tremendous opportunities for businesses that pay attention to their needs.

African-American businesses in the Fort Wayne MSA are predominately located in Allen County. By far the largest group of businesses owned by African Americans is in the service industry (excluding membership organizations and private households), and a large majority appear to have no employees. The data did not give the sales volume for each company; however Black-owned companies appear to fall into the category including the smallest number of employees. This may suggest that many African-Americans that go into business are developing an informal entrepreneurial skill. Further, African-American businesses as a whole as compared to White businesses appear not to have their sales and receipts documented for public record. This may suggest that the companies did not handle their financial information correctly; or that the information was not recorded properly by the reporting institution, or both. This problem may stem from having inadequate resources to perform basic accounting functions for the businesses. In any case, lack of proper documentation will make a company less bankable, which could have severe repercussions on its ability to secure loans or a line of credit in order to grow.

RECOMMENDATION

Marketers should start to put more emphasis on segmenting the African-American population. Because of differences in per capita income, wealth, demographics, and culture, the spending habits of African-Americans as a group are not the same as those of the average U.S. consumer. The most recent Consumer Expenditure Survey carried out by the U.S. Bureau of Labor Statistics (based on data from 1995) indicates that Black households spent only about 74 percent as much as the average U.S. household and spent a higher proportion of their after-tax income on goods and services. The values are based on money income, which differs somewhat from total buying power, but nonetheless this will offer businesses some insights into spending by Black consumers.

The service industry is growing fast in Northeast Indiana. Service businesses often lack the hard assets that a lending institution would like to see on financial statements. Therefore, resources should be available to help such companies identify ways of showing that they are growing and will be able to service their debts. Access to capital will be critical for these growing companies, fuel they will need in order to keep moving forward. It appears that business owners have the girth to start and run a business that will increase our tax base, potentially employ people and create a sense of pride in our community; which will put money back into the community. However, money doesn't solve all a company's woes. We must continue to provide resources that will deliver quality technical assistance to budding African-American firms. African-Americans in business in Fort Wayne seem to have the entrepreneur spirit and to have developed strengths as well as weaknesses in their quest to live the American dream. Entrepreneurs desire responsibility, have a preference for moderate risk, and are confident in their ability to succeed. Further, they desire immediate feedback, and they have a high level of energy. But by being the only one doing a multitude of tasks in the organization, an entrepreneur may get spread too thin in a company and thus be unable to grow his or her company to its maximum potential. If we can provide the proper assistance for Entrepreneurs needing assistance in small business accounting, management and financial analysis, we may be able to take advantage of a unique opportunity in our community that could jumpstart our economy for years to come.

Chapter 6: Education

Ruby Cain • Sherri Emerson • Dr. Shirley Hollis • Verleasish Jones • Greg Smith

INTRODUCTION

At no other time in America's history has an individual's education been so pivotal in his/her ability to obtain and sustain employment in a viable career and, subsequently, to contribute positively to the economic well-being of the community. To respond to the demands of industry in the Twenty-first Century, academic skills need to be more technically oriented and more flexible to industry change. Education must foster creative problem solving, independent decision-making, and collaboration. Because the stakes are far higher than in the past, success in employment is more dependent on access to quality education, a fact that promises to be a particular challenge to the African-American community. While there is general agreement that a racial gap in academic achievement plagues students in Fort Wayne and across the nation, that is where consensus ends. This chapter will give readers an overview of the following areas in education: The Achievement Gap, staff and student composition throughout EACS, FWCS, SWCS, and NWCS, data on I-STEP testing, graduation and drop out rates, discipline & school suspensions, teacher experience and qualifications, and the makeup of special education classes throughout the school systems in Fort Wayne. This information will give the community a better sense of what issues and problems need to be addressed for African-Americans throughout the Fort Wayne community in the area of education.

What follows is an exploration of local, regional, and national research applied to specific conditions in Fort Wayne. In the interest of time, the focus has been given to K-12 public education with the assumption that in-depth analysis of these data can shed light on other key indicators of the racial achievement gap that are outside the scope of the current assessments of educational success. The report is divided into four sections: The Achievement Gap: An Overview; The Assessment Model; Findings and Discussion; and Conclusions.

THE ACHIEVEMENT GAP: AN OVERVIEW

Despite decades of attention, the gap in academic achievement between students of color and their White counterparts remains one of the American education system's most pressing problems. Although the gap declined in most parts of the country in the 1970s and '80s, presumably related to the desegregation of schools in the 1950s and 1960s, it again widened in the 1990s (Haycock 2002; Jencks and Phillips 1998; Kober 2001; NCES 2001). The movement toward school desegregation lagged in Fort Wayne; it was not until the late 1980s that Fort Wayne Community Schools (FWCS) began systematic desegregation. In stark contrast to the national trend, there was no corresponding decline in the

achievement gap in Fort Wayne in the decade following desegregation. Although, the realization that the achievement gap is widening has prompted renewed public and political pressure for the education system to narrow the gap, it is clear that there has been a tendency by mainstream politicians and

KEY FINDINGS

- Over-representation of African-American students in the population of low achievers, as evidenced by I-Step scores, SAT scores, and GPA.

- Over-representation of African-American students in the population subjected to disciplinary action, as evidenced by rate of suspensions, expulsions, and other disciplinary actions.

- Under-representation of African-Americans as teachers, specifically, and certified staff, generally, has worsened over the last ten years, in spite of the fact that Fort Wayne/Allen County has become a more racially diverse community and the percentage of African-American students in particular has increased.

- The four school districts in Fort Wayne, like others across the country, may operate under a system of institutional racism that is less easily identified and more subtle but no less harmful to our students than individual acts of racism.

educators especially White educators to avoid looking to the school system and society at large for an explanation for the gap's existence and its worsening condition (Uhlenberg and Brown 2002). Rather, the tendency has been to explain the gap in terms of poor character, broken families, cultural dysfunction (Viadero 2000) and poverty, and often discussion appears to be aimed at minimizing its importance.

Various studies have reliably dispelled the notion that culture or character explains educational excellence or failure. Claims that the achievement gap is rooted in poverty continue to dominate much of the discussion about the racial divide. Nonetheless, it is important to note that there is overwhelming support for the claim that "poverty can't explain all of the achievement gap . . . because grade and test-score disparities crop up even in middle-class communities with integrated schools" (Johnson and Viadero 2000: 5; see also Haycock 2002). This is further supported by the fact that the gap is little better when Black and White children attend the same schools or when Black and White families have similar educations, earn roughly the same incomes, and hold about the same wealth (Jencks and Phillips 1998). Locally, statistics comparing the achievement of White and non-White students indicate that Fort Wayne students fare no better than their counterparts nationwide. In spite of the fact that local officials often claim to have made substantial

progress toward solving the problem (e.g. Fletcher 2002; Fowler-Finn 2001; Sadowski 2001), even a cursory review of published data strongly suggests that the achievement gap between African-American students and their White counterparts is yet significant in most, if not all, public schools in Fort Wayne and the surrounding area (see Table 1). More specifically, Fort Wayne Community Schools ISTEP data over several years (Table 2a) provides evidence that, although improvements have been made in some sectors, the achievement gap persists and, in fact, has worsened in some cases. East Allen County Schools (Table 2b) showed similar results in evidence of improvements, but even greater disparities in the achievement gap. Although there have been a small

reported, disparities can also be seen for Southwest Allen County Schools (Table 2c). It is important to note that the achievement gap widens from 3rd to 10th grade for the three school districts.

Fort Wayne, which encompasses all or part of 5 townships (Adams, Pleasant, St. Joseph, Washington, and Wayne), has students distributed across four school districts. As a whole the city, which is home to almost two-thirds of Allen County's 332,000 residents, is racially and ethnically diverse, and in 2000 African-Americans comprised 17.4 percent of Fort Wayne's total population of approximately 206,000, in contrast to 11.3 percent of the county's residents, 7.5 percent of the residents of the five county MSA area,

Table 1. Student Personal Development, Attainment, and Progress

	Racial Groups	% w/ High GPA*	% Enrolling in College	% Enrolled in Advanced Classes	% Enrolled in Special Education Classes	Average SAT Scores		% Passing ISTEP	
						Verbal*	Math*	Language Arts	Math
EACS	White		71%	0.91%				78%	73%
	Black			0.52%	21.19%			33%	19%
FWCS	White	14.8%	71%	4.89%	NA	513	508	72%	64%
	Black	1.7%		0.49%	NA	423	405	30%	23%
NACS	White		100%	2.37%	28.27%			84%	86%
	Black			NA	NA			NA	NA
SACS	White		87%	NA	NA			88%	85%
	Black			NA	NA			NA	NA

Sources: National Center for Educational Statistics, 2001;
*=various FWCS internal reports provided by corporation administration.
**= Indiana Department of Education, K-12 School Data, Corporation Snapshot.

decline in the percentages of those students passing the ISTEP, there is much progress to made within our local school systems.

Because ISTEP data is suppressed in groups with less than 10 students, comparisons between Black and White performances were not available for all grades at Southwest Allen County Schools and were not available for any grades at Northwest Allen County Schools. For the grades

and 8.4 percent of the residents of the state. Furthermore, while the African-American population is increasing at a faster rate than the white population, the Fort Wayne area is also becoming home to a rapidly increasing number of immigrants from around the world. Not surprisingly, while the White population in Fort Wayne and the surrounding area increased between 1980 and 2000 by 6.4 percent, the number of non-White residents has increased at a much faster rate

Table 2a. FWCS Yearly Comparison of % Passing ISTEP (NR = data suppressed for less than 10 students)								
Grade		% Passing ISTEP Lang Arts 1998-99	% Passing ISTEP Lang Arts 1999-00	% Passing ISTEP Lang Arts 2000-01	% Passing ISTEP Lang Arts 2001-02	% Passing ISTEP Math 1998-99	% Passing ISTEP Math 1999-00	% Passing ISTEP Math 2000-01	% Passing ISTEP Math 2001-02
3	White	68%	69%	66%	71%	71%	73%	75%	79%
	Black	33%	40%	33%	40%	39%	47%	45%	51%
6	White	58%	52%	50%	55%	56%	54%	60%	60%
	Black	24%	22%	17%	20%	20%	21%	25%	21%
8	White	71%	68%	71%	69%	63%	63%	66%	68%
	Black	38%	32%	39%	40%	23%	23%	29%	38%
10	White	76%	73%	73%	72%	59%	62%	65%	64%
	Black	39%	34%	33%	30%	19%	20%	28%	23%

Table 2b. EACS Yearly Comparison of % Passing ISTEP (NR = data suppressed for less than 10 students)								
Grade		% Passing ISTEP Lang. Arts 1998-99	% Passing ISTEP Lang. Arts 1999-00	% Passing ISTEP Lang Arts 2000-01	% Passing ISTEP Lang Arts 2001-02	% Passing ISTEP Math 1998-99	% Passing ISTEP Math 1999-2000	% Passing ISTEP Math 2000-01	% Passing ISTEP Math 2001-02
3	White	69%	72%	68%	70%	74%	75%	79%	75%
	Black	32%	30%	37%	32%	46%	43%	61%	40%
6	White	65%	63%	59%	62%	67%	61%	73%	71%
	Black	20%	20%	18%	13%	23%	19%	28%	24%
8	White	73%	75%	72%	74%	66%	67%	63%	67%
	Black	30%	23%	42%	36%	15%	14%	18%	19%
10	White	83%	83%	78%	78%	73%	73%	75%	73%
	Black	44%	44%	38%	33%	25%	24%	25%	19%

Table 2c. SACS Yearly Comparison of % Passing ISTEP (NR = data suppressed for less than 10 students)								
Grade		% Passing ISTEP Lang. Arts 1998-99	% Passing ISTEP Lang. Arts 1999-00	% Passing ISTEP Lang Arts 2000-01	% Passing ISTEP Lang Arts 2001-02	% Passing ISTEP Math 1998-99	% Passing ISTEP Math 1999-2000	% Passing ISTEP Math 2000-01	% Passing ISTEP Math 2001-02
3	White	83%	84%	82%	NR*	88%	89%	90%	NR*
	Black	NR	70%	NR	NR*	NR	70%	NR	NR*
6	White	79%	76%	72%	77%	82%	83%	82%	81%
	Black	40%	45%	50%	NR	60%	45%	50%	NR
8	White	88%	89%	90%	88%	90%	85%	86%	89%
	Black	NR	NR	77%	64%	NR	NR	77%	73%
10	White	92%	91%	89%	88%	87%	88%	89%	85%
	Black	NR	NR	NR	NR	NR	NR	NR	NR

*Note: In 2001-02 of the 473 students tested in Grade 3, only 1 reported ethnicity.

Table 2d. NACS Yearly Comparison of % Passing ISTEP (NR = data suppressed for less than 10 students)								
Grade		% Passing ISTEP Lang. Arts 1998-99	% Passing ISTEP Lang. Arts 1999-00	% Passing ISTEP Lang Arts 2000-01	% Passing ISTEP Lang Arts 2001-02	% Passing ISTEP Math 1998-99	% Passing ISTEP Math 1999-2000	% Passing ISTEP Math 2000-01	% Passing ISTEP Math 2001-02
3	White	76%	77%	70%	80%	83%	79%	85%	80%
	Black	NR	NR	NR	NR	NR	NR	NR	NR
6	White	74%	72%	70%	71%	74%	78%	80%	80%
	Black	NR	NR	NR	NR	NR	NR	NR	NR
8	White	81%	77%	78%	78%	80%	81%	76%	80%
	Black	NR	NR	NR	NR	NR	NR	NR	NR
10	White	85%	86%	85%	84%	80%	85%	84%	86%
	Black	NR	NR	NR	NR	NR	NR	NR	NR

Source: Indiana Department of Education, FWCS K-12 school data

(Hispanics by 162.0 percent; African Americans by 42.9 percent; and Asians by 221.7 percent) (see Table 3), mirroring a national trend. In fact, nearly 90 percent of the total growth in the U.S. population between 1995 and 2050 is expected to be among minority populations, and, by 2050, the White population will almost certainly have become the new numerical minority (He and Hobbs 1999). As a result, the school systems are no longer dealing with just Black and White issues, but with multi racial and ethnicity issues in the student population. Yet with the increased diversity, Fort Wayne remains the second most residentially segregated community in Indiana (Gruss and Shawgo 2001). The increased population diversity has not resulted in a corresponding increase in teacher diversity.

This topic will be explored later in this chapter. A second difficulty in assessing the racial gap in educational achievement in local schools relates to the fact that the 75 percent of Fort Wayne students who attend public schools are assigned to schools in one of four public school districts that together include 56 elementary, 16 middle and 11 high schools as well as 3 middle/high school combinations and 5 specialty schools, all of varying academic performance depending largely on the district in which they are found. Although the Fort Wayne Community School (FWCS) District is completely within the municipal boundaries and serves the largest share of the city's students, a significant number of students attend school in one of three districts that cross the city's boundaries: East Allen County Schools (EACS).

Northwest Allen County Schools (NACS), and Southwest Allen County Schools (SACS). The four Allen County districts differ demographically in a number of ways, particularly socio-economically and racially (see Table 4), a fact that makes solving the racial and ethnic achievement gaps in the public schools all the more urgent and difficult.

MEASURING THE ACHIEVEMENT GAP

Why is there such an alarming difference in performance between students who attend the same school?

Table 3. Ethnic and Racial Distribution of Population (Fort Wayne MSA)

	1980		1990		1980 -1990	2000		1980 -2000
	Number	Percent	Number	Percent	% Change	Number	Percent	% Change
Tot. Population	444,772	100.0%	456,281	100.0%	2.6%	502,141	100.0%	12.9%
Tot. Hispanics	6,377	1.4%	7,621	1.7%	19.5%	16,707	3.3%	162.0%
White*	408,751	91.9%	413,982	90.7%	1.3%	435,024	86.6%	6.4%
Black*	26,218	5.9%	30,205	6.6%	15.2%	37,456	7.5%	42.9%
Am. Indian*	789	0.2%	1,223	0.3%	55.0%	1,420	0.3%	80.0%
Asian*	1,559	0.4%	2,874	0.6%	84.4%	5,016	1.0%	221.7%
Other*	1,078	0.2%	376	0.1%	-65.1%	620	0.1%	-42.5%
Two or More Races*	NA	NA	NA	NA	NA	5,746	1.1%	

* Non-Hispanic only; in 1980 and 1990 "Asians" includes Hawaiians and Pacific Islanders.
Source: Census 2000 analyzed by the Social Science Data Analysis Network (SSDAN).

Researching the racial achievement gap is made difficult by the fact that attention up to this point has been largely focused on the gap and its symptoms but less on the conditions that cause it. Nationwide, this trend has been met with an increasing commitment to using verifiable data to draw attention to the achievement gap as one of the *effects* of discrimination and institutional racism (Spriggs 1999). The difficulty with this task arises when we attempt to isolate the particular behaviors, policies, practices, and conditions that combine to create the system of institutional inequality.

The National Task Force on Minority High Achievement suggests that research-validated, learner-centered principles must be used if we are to begin closing the racial achievement gap (McCombs 2000: 35). Furthermore, these research principles have the power to help us better understand why the gap exists, an essential step to solving the problem. However, success with such an approach rests on an ongoing institutional process of rigidly structured outcome assessments and an acknowledgement that "learning is most effective when differences in learners' linguistic, cultural, and social backgrounds are taken into account" (ibid).

Table 4. Socioeconomic and Racial/Ethnic Characteristics of Students by District, 2001-02

District	Public School Enrollment (2002-03)	Minority Public School Enrollment (2002-03)	% Minority Enrollment (2002-03)	Average Per Capita Income (1989)	% Families Living Below Poverty Level (1990)	% Students Receiving Free Lunch & Textbooks** (2001-02)
EACS	9,731	2,294	23.6%	$12,865	5.3%	31.0%
FWCS	32,081	12,027	37.5%	$13,568	10.7%	47.0%
NACS	4,791	273	5.7%	$17,828	1.5%	7.0%
SACS	5,874	511	8.7%	$25,993	1.4%	3.0%

** District-wide
Source: Indiana Department of Education, School Data, Corporation Snapshot, Population Characteristics

This initial assessment of racial inequality in educational achievement and the conditions related to it applies social scientific research methods to the evaluation of the achievement levels of Fort Wayne students. Newly developed data will be needed if we are to fully understand the problem at hand. We have extracted these data from reports submitted by the local school districts to the Indiana Department of Education and the National Center for Educational Statistics, both neutral, non-partisan agencies whose data are accepted as valid and reliable.

THE ASSESSMENT MODEL

Understanding the role that various aspects of the education system play in student achievement and the creation of gaps in achievement is an important step in the road toward developing meaningful policies and interventions. The current model, only briefly discussed here, is suggested by the research of the Commission for Racial Equality (CRE), which, in its 1997 "Exclusion from School and Racial Equality: A Good Practice Guide," outlined best practices for schools and local education authorities to use in assessing their programs and considering policy changes. As a starting point in what is by necessity an on-going assessment of area schools, these best practices provide us with both a conceptual framework for analyzing the available data and a map of future research needs. Table 5 provides a detailed set of indicators and measures that are suggested as useful in identifying the causes of the achievement gap.

FINDINGS AND DISCUSSION

Based on the CRE assessment model, we have identified specific areas for which data is currently available and accessible. We begin our initial evaluation with those aspects of the local school districts while recognizing the need to expand our assessment to include other data if we are to inform adequately the discussion on closing

Table 5. Education Assessment Indicators and Measures

Area of Interest	Indicators	Suggested Measures
Policy, Leadership, and Management	Segregation Policies	□ Rate of within-district segregation □ Rate of between-district segregation □ Discrepancy between the proportion of minority and non-minority students enrolled in private and parochial schools
	Investment in Education	□ Discrepancy between the average expenditures per student in predominantly minority and non-minority schools □ Discrepancy between the average student-to-computer ratio in predominantly minority and non-minority schools. □ Discrepancy between average number of contemporary (less than 5 years old) library books per student in predominantly minority and non-minority schools □ Discrepancy between teacher-student ratio in predominantly minority and non-minority schools/classes
	Assessment Policies	□ Extent to which student promotion decisions are based on high-stakes tests □ Application of assessment techniques based on alternative achievement factors
	Orientation of School Leadership & Management	□ Discrepancy between the proportion of leaders' attention focused clearly on major priorities, interests, and commitments of the corporation in predominantly minority and non-minority schools □ Discrepancy between the proportion of district goals that are clearly derived from the overall mission of the school district in predominantly minority and non-minority schools □ Extent to which activities of administrators model the particular behaviors necessary to meet the goals and fulfill the mission of the school corporation
Staff Recruitment, Training, and Professional Development	Teacher Qualifications	□ Discrepancy between the average teachers' tenure in predominantly minority and non-minority schools □ Discrepancy between the proportion of minority and non-minority students taught by teachers without a major or minor in the subject area they teach □ Discrepancy between the proportion of minority and non-minority students taught by teachers who are fully licensed/ certified □ Discrepancy between the proportion of minority and non-minority students taught by teachers with emergency licenses □ Discrepancy between the proportion of minority and non-minority students taught by out-of-field teachers □ Extent to which district reports teacher qualifications to the public
	Teacher Performance	□ Discrepancy between the teachers' effectiveness at working with minority and non-minority students □ Discrepancy between the teachers' effectiveness at working with minority and non-minority parents □ Discrepancy between the teachers' effectiveness at working with minority and non-minority staff □ Measurable evidence of teachers' professional growth in understanding of diversity □ Use of objective review of teachers' performance based on clearly defined standards that are strongly related to the district's mission and goals.
	Racial Diversity	□ Discrepancy between majorities and minorities as a proportion of teaching faculty and the student body.
Curriculum, Teaching, and Assessment		□ Discrepancy between the proportion of minority and non-minority students enrolled in advance placement/honors classes □ Discrepancy between the proportion of minority and non-minority students enrolled in special education □ Discrepancy between the proportion of minority and non-minority students enrolled in remedial education because of low achievement □ Discrepancy between the proportion of minority and non-minority students receiving failing grades □ Discrepancy between the proportion of minority and non-minority students who fail to be promoted □ Reliance on problem-based or project-based learning vs. curriculum aimed at students passing knowledge-based tests (Newell 2002)
Discipline and Exclusion		□ Discrepancy between the proportion of minority and non-minority students receiving rewards vs. punishment in response to discipline problems. □ Discrepancy between the proportion of minority and non-minority students expelled or suspended from school
Parental Relations and Community Partnerships		□ Discrepancy between the proportion of minority and non-minority parents encouraged to become actively involved in school activities □ Discrepancy between the relations of teachers and administration with minority and non-minority communities. □ Discrepancy between teacher and administration relationships with minority and non-minority parents.
School Environment and Student Attitudes		□ Discrepancy between proportion of minority and non-minority students who report being fairly treated by teachers and administrators □ Discrepancy between proportion of minority and non-minority students who report feeling isolated

POLICY, LEADERSHIP, AND MANAGEMENT

Research shows that a number of policies create and maintain the racial achievement gap. These include, among other factors, school segregation, investment in education, and the orientation of school leadership and management, all of which will be discussed here in the preliminary assessment of education policies of the four school districts being examined.

SEGREGATION

The increase in school segregation in the 1990's has led at least one scholar to connect these trends to the widening gap in academic achievement between students of color and their White counterparts (Orfield 2001). Although many others tend to treat segregation as a phenomenon involving the isolation of racial groups from each other within schools and school districts, it takes other forms that are more often overlooked. These include high levels of private and parochial school enrollment to the exclusion of investment in public schools as well as de facto residential segregation related to the out-migration of Whites from urban areas. Both factors are legacies of an earlier era that have survived the 1980s reorganization in Fort Wayne Schools nominally aimed at ending legal segregation and decreasing levels of racial isolation and inequality.

Nearly a quarter of the students in the city of Fort Wayne attend non-public schools, an especially high

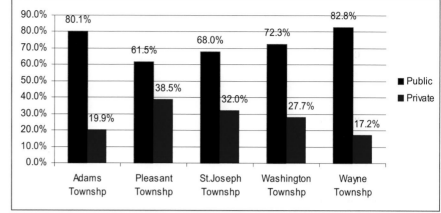

Figure 1. Students in Public and Private School by Township

Source: U.S. Census Bureau, Census 2000 Summary File 1, Matrix P8

rate compared to the 10 percent of elementary and secondary students enrolled in private and parochial schools across the U.S. overall. In Fort Wayne, the private sector of the school population includes students enrolled in 15 Catholic Diocese of Fort Wayne schools, 25 Lutheran schools, 6 Amish schools and a number of other non-parochial, non-public schools of various types. Whether students are educated in public or non-public schools varies significantly across the Fort Wayne metropolitan area and is heavily influenced by race, ethnicity, and socioeconomic status. In fact, the two townships (see Fig. 1) with the lowest concentrations of students attending non-public schools are Adams and Wayne, which also have the highest concentration of African-American families in the city.

The de facto segregation in area schools is particularly troublesome when one considers that, although FWCS serves a population with the highest aggregate number of minority students, the schools with the highest proportion of minorities enrolled are actually in EACS (NCES 2001). These students live mostly in the

southeast quadrant of the city, home to a large portion of the city's African American residents, and attend Village Elementary (which is 82% African American), Prince Chapman Academy (78% African American), or Paul Harding High School (79% African American), reminiscent of the conditions that existed across much of the country prior to desegregation.

Importantly, the racial distribution found in EACS is similar to conditions found by the U.S. Office of Civil Rights in a 1969 site review

Table 6. Average Expenditures per Student by District (3 yr avg.) 2000-01

District	Expenditures
EACS	$ 7,500
FWCS	$ 7,800
NACS	$ 6,700
SACS	$ 9,100

NR = Not Reported.
Source: Indiana Department of Education, School Data 2000-01, Corporation Snapshot, Population Characteristics

of FWCS when they revealed "several possible Title VI violations, including discriminatory student and teacher assignment practices" (Equal Opportunity 1979: 11). When the 1977 reassessment of FWCS by the Indiana Advisory Committee to the U.S. Commission on Civil Rights found that "racial isolation in the FWCS had been steadily increasing for several years," closer monitoring of FWCS followed. Dissatisfied with the progress made, a group calling itself Parents for Quality Education with Integration (PQEI) filed suit in 1986 in federal court and reached a settlement 1989 with FWCS that promised to work toward racial balance (How it Happened, 1998). A similar action taken against EACS failed (Boggs 1993).

A number of factors are involved in White losses in urban school districts among which are opportunities available to White students in other schools and districts to reduce contact with the non-White populations (Clotfelter 2001). These opportunities are created for suburban children in two ways: enrollment in private and parochial schools and between-district segregation. Private schools have clearly played a role in the racial segregation of students in grades K-12 during the past 40 years; however, because of White flight out of urban areas, de facto segregation has contributed directly to factors creating the racial achievement gap in public schools across district lines. Furthermore, as White students have been moved out of urban schools, there has been marked disinvestment in those schools and other urban services (Delgado 1999).

INVESTMENT IN EDUCATION

A significant portion of the overall tax in most school districts goes to support public schools. Although the Indiana Department of Education claims, "Indiana has one of the most

successful school funding formulas in the country" (Theobald 2001), the difference in wealth helps to explain the greater per child investment in education in some districts as compared to others (see Table 6). Southwest Allen County Schools has experienced the most rapid growth in net assessed property value (11.87%) while the weakest growth was in the East Allen County School District (2.66%). While the tax rates increased at a fairly uniform rate across the four districts, SACS had the fastest growth in overall tax levies (10.15%) in contrast to EACS's growth of 0.74% (ACEDC 1997). These data reflect two conditions. First, the median value for a residential dwelling in Aboite Township, where students attend SACS, is $146,700 in comparison to $74,200 in Adams Township, where most students attend EACS. And second, SACS and NACS both of which service the western part of Allen County, has experienced that fastest growth rate in new property development and property value in the area.

INSTITUTIONAL RACISM

One of many scholarly perspectives on the racial gap in school achievement points to a system of institutional racism as being at the root of the achievement gap. "Institutional racism has been defined as a system of power based on race that gives advantages to White people at the expense of people of color. It is historically based and can be perpetuated with or without intention or awareness." (Applied Research Center http://arc.org/). It is a

historically based set of social arrangements, that operate in such a way that they permit, encourage, or sustain the fact that because of their race specific groups in society are denied the opportunity to have equal access to those material and nonmaterial effects that are necessary for mobility in a class society (Knowles and Prewett 1969). Institutional racism can be assessed through curricula, instructional strategies and teaching styles that are incompatible with a Black student's cultural preferences; absence of materials which include Black content and role models; stereotyping and the resulting low or negative teacher expectations; academic tracking and the resulting failure to foster higher order thinking skills; and test bias (Kuykendall 1991).

THE EDUCATIONAL ENVIRONMENT

Recent data of not only student achievement but also of a range of classroom and institutional practices allow scholars to study how different factors influence student outcomes. It also shows with clarity the impact of the educational environment on student outcomes (Wenglinsky 2001). The educational environment is directly influenced by a number of factors including teacher performance and lack of qualifications. There is also significant evidence that the expectations teachers have of their students are good indicators of how well the students actually perform (Ferguson 1998). Importantly, few states and districts have designed specific policy strategies to address these problems as a way of closing the achievement gap (Ansell and McCabe 2003; Kozol 1991; Sadowski 2001).

TEACHER QUALIFICATIONS AND PERFORMANCE

A lack of diversity and a high proportion of students from poor families are often viewed as contributing to low academic performance. Other contributing factors include teacher qualifications and performance. Importantly, many of these students themselves recognize the fact that their teachers are often lacking in knowledge about subjects being taught (Haycock, 2001). These students are less likely than others to be taught by teachers trained in their subjects, teachers who have had professional development in high-order thinking skills, and those trained in awareness about issues related to student racial, cultural, and socioeconomic diversity (ibid.). Data to assess adequately was not readily available to this chapter's authors. We know only that most teachers (in Fort Wayne's public school districts) meet the state's minimum certification standards.

RACIAL DIVERSITY

The importance of racial diversity among faculty and staff impact two aspects of the educational climate. On one hand, the presence of teachers and staff that represent the student body's racial and ethnic diversity is important in the creation of positive role models and an increased level of understanding of the unique conditions that certain

populations of children face. However, poor students and students of color are more likely than White middle and upper class students to be taught by school personnel who are of a different racial, ethnic, or socioeconomic group than their own (Chaika 2001), and only a smaller proportion of the faculty and staff in

the various districts are minorities, especially when compared to the minority to White student ratio. According to U.S. Department of Commerce data, more than one-third of those enrolled in today's public schools are students of color, and, by 2025 that proportion is expected to reach at least half. Meanwhile, only 13 percent of their teachers are

minority, and more than 40 percent of schools across America have no teachers of color on staff (cited in NEA 2002).

The research of Gary Orfield, who played a pivotal role in the desegregation of Fort Wayne Community Schools, and his

associates at the Harvard University Civil Rights Project has shown that "racial segregation almost always accompanies segregation by poverty and many forms of related inequality. Levels of competition among students and parent support are much lower in schools with fewer resources. Qualified and experienced teachers often leave such schools."

Table 7a. Comparison of Racial Diversity of Certified Employees by District, 1991-92 vs. 2002-03

District	% Minority Enrollment (1991-92)	% Minority Enrollment (2002-03)	Certified Employees* (F.T.E.) (1991-92)	Certified Employees* (F.T.E.) (2002-03)	# Minority Certified Employees* (1991-92)	# Minority Certified Employees* (2002-03)	% Minority Certified Employees* (1991-92)	% Minority Certified Employees* (2002-03)
EACS	14.7%	23.6%	595.9	656.5	13.3	30.0	2.2%	4.6%
FWCS	27.0%	37.5%	1,867.9	2,015.0	199.0	216.0	10.7%	10.7%
NACS	1.7%	5.7%	171.7	307.7	1.0	1.0	0.6%	0.3%
SACS	3.2%	8.7%	296.8	403.5	1.0	4.0	0.3%	1.0%
GARY	98.7%	99.3%	1663.2	1314.7	1235.7	1091.3	74.3%	83.0%

* Certified employees may be teachers, administrators, counselors, or staff.
Source: Indiana Department of Education, School Data, Corporation Snapshot, Population Characteristics

Table 7b. 10 Year Comparison of Minority Certified Employees and Students

	Minority Certified Employees		Minority Students	
	1992-03	2002-03	1992-03	2002-03
EACS	2.6%	4.6%	15.5%	23.6%
FWCS	10.7%	10.7%	27.4%	38.4%
NACS	0.5%	0.3%	1.9%	6.2%
SACS	0.3%	1.0%	3.4%	9.2%
GARY	74.4%	83.0%	98.6%	99.3%

Source: Indiana Department of Education School Population Characteristics

Table 7c. 2003 Teachers and Students by Race/Ethnicity

Corporation	Black		White	
	Teachers	Students	Teachers	Students
EACS	3.0%	<24%*	96.0%	76.0%
FWCS	7.0%	< 37%*	91.0%	63.0%
NACS	0%	< 6%*	100%	94.0%
SACS	0%	< 8%*	98%	91.0%
GARY+	72%	< 9%*	24.0%	1.0%
All Indiana Public Schools (does not include charter schools)	3.9%	< 19.5%*	95.0%	80.5%

Source: Indiana Department of Education
* Percentage displayed is for minority students in total, however the majority of these students are African-American/Black
+ GARY statistics provided for comparison purposes only

(Frankenberg, Lee, and Orfield 2003:11). This has important implications since, as research indicates, "both Black and White children score higher on mathematics and reading tests when their teachers are the same race as they are" (Viadero 2001). Our data reveals a significant difference between the proportion of minorities found among the student population and the teachers across all four school districts in Fort Wayne (see Tables 7a - 7c). Although data on minority certified employees is provided by Indiana Department of Education, the number of minority teachers (see Table 7c) is a smaller subset of that number. In Fort Wayne Community Schools only 61% of the minority certified employees are Black teachers in the classroom (other minority teachers are 15% of the of the minority certified employees). The Indiana Department of Education's omission of the number or ratio of minority teachers in the Population Characteristics and Performance Report data may be indicative of their failure to acknowledge race and ethnicity as important indicators of success in eliminating the achievement gap.

The lack of progress made in the last decade in increasing the percentage of minority teachers by all four school districts is not sufficient. In comparison, Gary (IN) Community School Corporation, which is only 137 miles from Fort Wayne and has a much higher percentage of students of families in poverty, has increased minority certified employees from 74.3% to 83.0% while the minority student population increased from 98.7% to 99.3%. This suggests that

if this particular problem is to be solved aggressive recruiting from surrounding areas, some as close as Gary, should replace the local district administrators concerns about their inability to compete for the shrinking pool of Black teachers with school systems in Chicago, Detroit, and Indianapolis. In addition, recruiting and retention strategies used in Gary should be evaluated for applicability to Fort Wayne.

LOW EXPECTATIONS

Both high and low expectations from leaders trickle down through the education system and have short- and long-term impacts on students of color (Johnston and Viadero 2000). A leading scholar (Ferguson) concludes that "teachers' perceptions, expectations and behaviors probably do help to sustain, and perhaps even expand, the Black-White test score gap" (Ferguson 1998:313). His research documents the fact that teachers have very different expectations and opinions of Black

students and White students and these gaps in expectations lead teachers to behave differently and, in turn, reinforce lower Black student performance. Ferguson also cites research that demonstrates that teachers tend on average to be less supportive of Black students, perhaps because of their lower expectations. And, because teachers are less supportive, their behaviors could be expected to cause the low performance that they already expect from their students—creating a "self-fulfilling prophecy." Furthermore, according to an American Federation of Teachers report, in the absence of satisfactory academic performance, grade promotion in spite of poor performance actually perpetuates academic failure by teaching students that effort and achievement are not important, that objective standards are not very objective, and grading standards are arbitrarily enforced (Shanker 1996). It should be noted that this is not solely a problem unique to White teachers.

Table 8. Enrollment in Advance Placement & Special Education Classes by Race/District

District	Race*	% in Advanced Classes[1]	% in Special Education Classes[2]
EACS	White	0.91%	NA
	Black	0.52%	21.19%
FWCS	White	4.89%	NA
	Black	0.49%	NA
NACS	White	2.37%	NA
	Black	NA	NA
SACS	White	NA	NA
	Black	NA	NA

* Not Hispanic   ** NA= not currently available or not reported by race.
Sources:
[1] National Center for Educational Statistics, 2001.
[2] Skiba et al. 2000. "Minority Overrepresentation in Indiana's Special Education Programs: A Status Report." Bloomington, IN: Indiana Department of Education Division of Special Education.

On the contrary, Ferguson (1998) reports that Black teachers often have similarly low expectations for Black students.

Importantly, having a higher proportion of Black students in a class may actually lead teachers to reduce their expectations for all Black students, regardless of their capabilities or performance (Hanushek, Kain, and Rivkin 2002).

CURRICULUM

The curriculum adopted in the school has a direct impact on student achievement and affects student differentially in a number of ways. First, schools often fail to teach multicultural issues or, when they do, assign to those responsibilities teachers who lack adequate preparation to address the topic (Ramsey and Gallos 1997). Second, different academic curricula are used with different sectors of the school population, often based less on abilities than expectations and "objective" assessments, and such tracking is widely recognized as a prevalent way poor students and students of color are disadvantaged (Fritzberg 2001). Two common forms of tracking are indicated by the number of students of color in advanced placement or honors courses. As Table 8 shows, a much higher proportion of White than Black students are enrolled in such courses. A more subtle indicator would be the number of students of color who are encouraged or discouraged from taking these courses. Conversely, there are indications that minorities are over-

represented in Indiana's Special Education Programs (Losen and Orfield 2002), including those in Allen County (Skiba et al. 2000).

DISCIPLINE AND EXCLUSION

While a majority of teachers, when asked how well prepared they feel they are to meet classroom demands, report feeling "very well prepared" to maintain classroom order and discipline. The 1998 National Center for Education Statistics show that teachers with three or fewer years of teaching experience were less likely to feel so well prepared (NCES 1999). Importantly and paradoxically, these are the educators most likely to be assigned to "problem" schools where maximum skills are needed, a fact that has important long-term consequences. For instance, the NCES study suggests that student behavioral problems are rooted in early aggressive behaviors occurring in poorly managed classrooms (see also Greer-Chase, Rhodes, Kellam 2002). Unfortunately, this often leads

to discipline problems being dealt with in ways that further alienate these students from the "normal" school experience. More and more schools have implemented "zero tolerance" policies that tend to increase the number of student suspensions and expulsions, all of which have been shown to do little to correct the problem but do a great deal to damage the affected students' future educational outlook (Holloway 2002). Furthermore research has also indicated that zero tolerance policies are more commonly found in school districts with large minority populations and that African-American students—and especially African-American male students— are more often and more severely disciplined in schools than White students (The Advancement Project and the Civil Rights Project 2000).

Evidence in the Fort Wayne schools indicates that that the racial discrepancy in punishment crosses most if not all sectors of the four local school systems (see Table 9).

Table 9. Suspensions & Expulsions by Race/District

District	Race**	Combined Suspensions & Expulsions	Out of School Suspensions	% Expulsions
EACS	Total	14.0%		
	White		6.26%	0.39%
	Black		18.65%	1.55%
FWCS	Total	28.3%		
	White		14.02%	2.34%
	Black		29.85%	4.55%
NACS	Total	3.4%		
	White		2.84%	0.47%
	Black		NA	NA
SACS	Total *	4.4%	NA	NA
	White	NA	NA	NA
	Black	NA	NA	NA

* Southwest Allen County Schools' data is not currently available
** Not Hispanic
Source: National Center for Educational Statistics, 2001.

In pursuing exemplary student achievement, one must understand that poor student behavior is often the "outcome of a predictable chain of events that begins with academic failure" (Scott, Nelson, Liaupsin 2001). Furthermore, there is strong evidence that efforts to prevent such behavior actually begin with schools promoting academic instruction and facilitating student success (ibid.).

In the past two years, officials from FWCS report that the gap in how Black and White students rate the school climate has narrowed by about 60 percent (Sadowski 2001). However, it remains true that many Black students feel less connected to school and are more likely to have poor relationships with teachers and peers than their White counterparts. Research indicates that Black students are also less likely to feel that school rules are clear and enforced fairly, and they tend to think that they are more readily punished and less frequently praised in school (Fletcher 2002). School climate is a reflection of the attitudes of student, faculty, and staff toward the institutional culture, which is the "shared philosophies, ideologies, values, assumptions, beliefs, expectations, attitudes, and norms that knit a community together" (Kilmann, Saxton, and Serpa 1985: 5).

CONCLUSIONS

Based on the data presented here, it appears that institutional racism still persists within our local school systems. Although institutional racism may be less easily identified and more subtle it is no less harmful to our students and community as a whole than individual acts of racism. Although most studies of institutional racism and low expectations have largely been based on anecdotal accounts that may or may not be accurate reflections of the experiences of the larger population, more recently, scholars, activists, and the public at large have come to accept that the *presence* of institutional racism may be established using official statistics such as those presented here. In doing so, we minimize the chance the problem can continue to be denied.

Significantly, there is extensive support for the claim that all "children can achieve when they are taught the basics early; when they are challenged by high standards and a rich curriculum; and when caring, firm adults pay strict attention to the quality of students' work and behavior" (Starr 1997). Furthermore, it has been proposed that closing the Black-White test score gap could possibly "do more to promote racial equality than any other strategy that commands broad political support" (Jencks and Phillips 1998).

It is our hope that the community will begin to assess the presence of behaviors, attitudes, and policies that systemically function so as to deprive Black children of a comparable education when compared to their White counterparts in local schools.

Chapter 7: CRIME AND JUSTICE

Thomas D. Stucky, Ph.D

INTRODUCTION

This chapter discusses a number of aspects of crime and criminal justice in Fort Wayne, including: trends in reported crime, arrest rates and characteristics of arrestees by age, race, and gender, demographic characteristics of the police force, characteristics of the local jail population, the number and type of citizen complaints against police and characteristics of citizen complainants, as well as reported bias or hate crimes. The discussion will focus primarily on current figures and trends for the city of Fort Wayne with comparisons to state and national trends whenever possible.

OVERALL CRIME PATTERNS 1985-2000

This section examines trends in the number of reported crimes in Fort Wayne. The most widely known source of information on crime in the United States comes from the Federal Bureau of Investigation (FBI). The FBI compiles local police reports of crime from all over the country on a monthly basis (Federal Bureau of Investigation, Crime in the United

States, 2000, http://www.fbi.gov/ucr/cius_00/00crime1.pdf). The FBI keeps track of the number of certain crimes reported to the police and the number of arrests for these crimes. These are known as the index crimes, which are divided into violent offenses and property offenses. The violent index offenses include: murder and non-negligent manslaughter, rape, robbery, and aggravated assault. The property index offenses include: burglary, larceny (theft), motor vehicle theft, and arson. The FBI also collects information from local police agencies on the number of arrests *only* for other types of crime, such as: drug offenses, gambling, minor assaults, domestic abuse, and fraud. This chapter focuses on the index offenses because these are usually considered to be the most serious and are the ones the public most often hears about in the media. This chapter refers to crime in terms of a rate that is often used in criminal justice. The rate per 100,00 residents is a way of making meaningful comparisons across places with different population sizes, and is the number of crimes one

would expect for each 100,000 residents in a city or given area. So, for example, if a town has 50,000 residents and 5 homicides, then the

KEY FINDINGS

- Violent crime rates in Fort Wayne are higher than the Indiana average but lower than the national average for cities of similar size.

- Data provided by the Citizens Complaint Office displayed a disproportionate number of complaints filed by African-Americans and women.

- The Allen County Court computer system should be updated and integrated with computers from the prosecutor's office. Currently it is extremely difficult to determine independently whether race or other extra-legal factors play a role in prosecutorial and sentencing decisions in Allen County because key case information is not computerized. In addition, information is not integrated between the prosecutor's office and the Allen County Court system, making it difficult to follow cases through the system.

- Hate crimes and or bias crimes are likely to occur more often than are reported to the police.

Figure 1. Trends in Reported Index Crime Rates, 1985-2000.

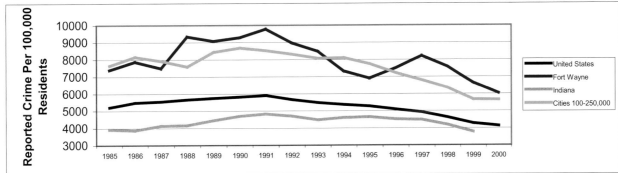

Source: Federal Bureau of Investigation, Crime in the United States, 1985-2000.

rate per 100,000 residents would be 10. This allows one to compare the amount of crime in Fort Wayne to large cities such as New York or Los Angeles in a meaningful way.

Figure 1 shows the overall rate of index crimes reported to police per 100,000 residents from 1985- 2000 for Fort Wayne, Indiana, national trends, and trends for cities with 100,000- 250,000 residents (Federal Bureau of Investigation, Crime in the United States, 1985-2000, Washington, DC: USGPO). During this period Fort Wayne experienced an increase in reported crime from 1985 through about 1991 and then a general decline through 2000 with a minor increase in 1997. The graph shows that the overall crime rate in Fort Wayne is higher than reported crime nationally and for the state of Indiana. The general trends are the same for each of the groups included in Figure 1. Each experienced an increase in reported crime through the early 1990s and then a decline. Fort Wayne averaged between 6,000 and 10,000 reported index offenses per 100,000 residents. The population of Fort Wayne was approximately 173,000 in 1990 and

grew to approximately 206,000 in 2000 (U.S. Census Bureau, Census of Population (1990, 2000), Washington, DC: USGPO). Therefore, the actual number of serious crimes reported to the police ranged from 11,000 to 17,000 annually. Although crime is higher in Fort Wayne than the national average and the Indiana average, the best comparison is probably between Fort Wayne and cities of similar size. The trend for cities with 100-250,000 residents fluctuates less from year to year because it averages across more than 100 cities. Figure 1 shows that the trends in reported serious crimes in Fort Wayne from 1985-2000 are very similar to other cities with a similar number of residents.

Figure 2 shows trends in reported *violent* crime rates per 100,000 residents for Fort Wayne and the comparison groups included in Figure 1. Consistent with overall crime rates, reported violent crime increased in Fort Wayne through about 1991 and then generally declined through the rest of the 1990s. However, the violent crime rate in Fort Wayne is consistently *below* the national average *and* the average for

comparably sized cities. Fort Wayne does have a somewhat higher violent crime rate than the Indiana average, especially from 1985 to 1992. Comparing the violent crime rate to cities with 100-250,000 residents shows that Fort Wayne's violent crime rate is 1/3 to 1/2 lower than the national average for cities of the same size from 1985 to 2000. Thus, Fort Wayne has similar reported crime rates to other cities of similar size across the country but a much lower violent crime rate. This indicates that, on average, a larger proportion of Fort Wayne's crimes are property crimes such as burglary and theft offenses.

Figure 3 shows the trends in reported homicide rates per 100,000 residents for Fort Wayne, Indiana, cities with 100,000 -250,000 residents and nationally from 1985-2000 (Federal Bureau of Investigation, Crime in the United States, 1985-2000, Washington, DC: USGPO). Fort Wayne experienced a decline in homicides from 1985 to 1987. Then, homicides increased from 1988 to 1994. The number of homicides decreased from 1995 through 2000 with the exception of an increase in

Figure 2. Trends in Reported Violent Crime Rates, 1985-2000

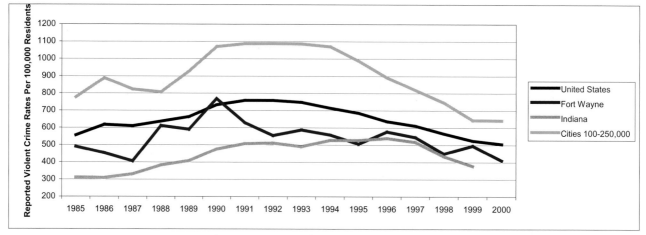

Source: Federal Bureau of Investigation, Crime in the United States, 1985-2000.

Figure 3. Trends in Reported Homicide Rates, 1985-2000

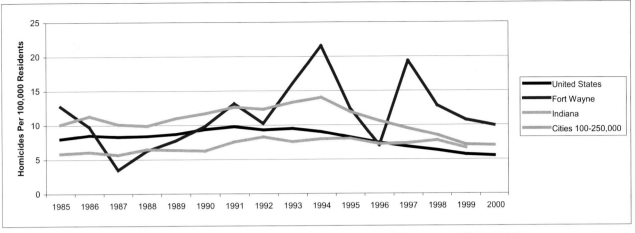

Source: Federal Bureau of Investigation, <u>Crime in the United States</u>, 1985-2000.

1997. From 1985 to 2000, the highest number of homicides in Fort Wayne occurred in 1994 (38) and the lowest was in 1987 (5). The average for the entire period was approximately 20 homicides per year. Figure 3 also shows that Fort Wayne had fewer homicides in relation to the number of residents than cities of similar size for the 1985 to 1990 period and with the exception of 1994 and 1997 experienced approximately similar homicide rates in the 1990s.

ARREST TRENDS 1990- 2001

The discussion to this point has focused on the number of crimes reported to the police. This section discusses arrest rates broken down by age, race, and gender. It is important to remember that not all reported crimes end in an arrest, and arrests do not always end in conviction. In fact, the percentage of crimes ending in arrest can be quite small depending on the type of crime. For instance, in the city of Fort Wayne during the 1990s only about 10%

of reported property crimes and about 20% of reported violent crimes ended in arrest (compiled from Fort Wayne Police Department (PD) unpublished data and FBI unpublished data). Therefore, one should be cautious about drawing conclusions regarding the characteristics of all criminals based on the characteristics of those that are arrested. However, the FBI arrest statistics are the only publicly available data that provides information on the race/ ethnicity, gender and age of criminals.

Figure 4. Percent of Adult Property Crime Arrests by Race, 1990-2001.

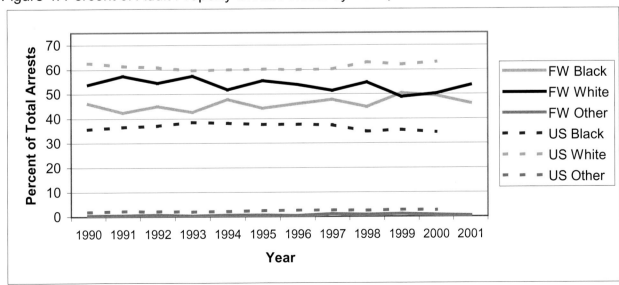

Source: Compiled from Fort Wayne Police Department unpublished data and FBI, <u>Crime in the United States</u>, 1990-2000.

The State of Black Fort Wayne • 2003

Figure 4 shows the percent of property crime (burglary, larceny, and motor vehicle theft) arrests accounted for by Whites and Blacks from 1990- 2001 for Fort Wayne and national trends for comparison (compiled from unpublished data from Fort Wayne PD and the FBI). In Fort Wayne Whites accounted for between 50 and 60% of property crime arrests from 1990- 2001, while Blacks accounted for between 40 and 50% of property crime arrests. Although the raw number of Whites arrested was higher, the *rate* of arrests was higher for African-Americans. If race were unrelated to the likelihood of arrest, we would expect that about 75% of arrestees would be White and about 17% would be African- American based on the percentage of residents of Fort Wayne in each racial group (U.S. Census Bureau, Census of Population (2000), http://factfinder.census.gov). Figure 4 shows that Asians and Native Americans (shown on the graph as the other category) account for less

than 3% of property crime arrests nationally. The percent of property crime arrests for Native Americans and Asians in Fort Wayne is even lower than the national average throughout the period, accounting for 1% or less of all property crime arrests from 1990- 2001. Rates of arrest for Blacks in Fort Wayne were higher than the national rate, while arrest rates for whites were lower than the national rates.

Figure 5 shows a similar breakdown for violent crime arrests from 1990- 2001. Blacks are more likely to be arrested for violent index offenses than Whites. During the 1990s Blacks accounted for between 55 and 70% of arrests for violent crimes (homicide, robbery, aggravated assault and rape), whereas Whites accounted for between 30 and 45% of arrests for violent index offenses. Therefore, Blacks are over-represented among violent crime arrestees in Fort Wayne. Similar to property crimes, Asians and Native Americans consistently account for less than 3% of violent crime arrests

nationally. However, the percent of violent crime arrests accounted for by Asians and Native Americans in Fort Wayne is consistently below the national average, peaking in 2001 at 1.6%.

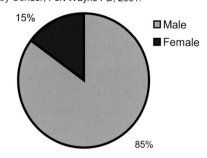

Figure 6. Percent of Adult Violent Crime Arrests by Gender, Fort Wayne PD, 2001.

15%

☐ Male
■ Female

85%

Source: compiled from Fort Wayne Police Department unpublished data.

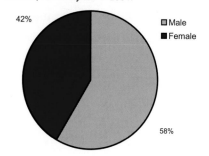

Figure 7. Percent of Property Crime Arrests by Gender, Fort Wayne PD 2001.

42%

☐ Male
■ Female

58%

Source: compiled from Fort Wayne Police Department unpublished data.

Figure 5. Percent of Adult Violent Crime Arrests by Race, 1990- 2001.

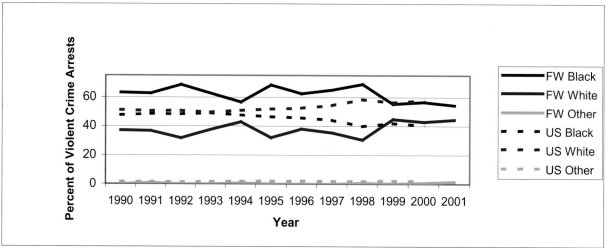

Source: Compiled from Fort Wayne Police Department unpublished data and FBI's Crime in the United States, 1990-2000.

The State of Black Fort Wayne • 2003

Figures 6 and 7 show the percentage of arrestees in Fort Wayne in 2001 broken down by gender (unpublished Fort Wayne PD data). Men make up slightly less than half of Fort Wayne's residents but account for 85% of arrests for violent crimes. Although long- term national trend data was not available, the current local arrest figures by gender are consistent with national figures. For example, in 2000 on the average, men made up about 82.3% of violent crime arrests (US Dept. of Justice, Table 48, Crime in the United States, 2000, Washington, DC: USGPO). However, the percent of female property crime arrests in Fort Wayne last year was much higher than the national average for cities. Forty-two percent of property crime arrestees in Fort Wayne in 2001 were female compared with a national average of only 31% of women arrestees for property offenses.

Figure 8 shows the percent of index offense arrests broken down by age groups in 2001 for the city of Fort Wayne and nationally. Young adults

in Fort Wayne are much more likely to be arrested than older residents. Arrests for property crime decreased consistently as Fort Wayne's residents got older. Violent crime arrests increased slightly when residents were in their late 20s and early 30s and declined after that. Residents over the age of 45 accounted for only about 10 percent of arrests for index offenses in 2001. These patterns are very consistent over time within the city and with national average crime rates by age (US Dept. of Justice, FBI, Table 38, Crime in the United States, 2001, Washington, DC: USGPO).

LAW ENFORCEMENT OFFICERS

This section discusses the composition of the Fort Wayne Police Department in 2002 and 1990. Table 1 provides a breakdown of the sworn police officers in Fort Wayne PD, by race/ethnicity and gender. In 1990 there were 307 sworn police officers (U.S. Bureau of Justice Statistics Law Enforcement Management and Administrative Statistics, 1990. By

2002 that number had increased nearly 25% to 380 sworn officers (unpublished Fort Wayne PD manpower report). In both 1990 and 2002, White males made up about 73% of the total number of sworn officers. The number of White female officers nearly doubled in 12 years from 18 to 31, although percentage increase was much less. White females made up 5.9% of sworn officers in 1990 and approximately 8.2% in 2002. The number of Black male sworn officers increased slightly from 41 in 1990 to 42 in 2002. However, the

Table 1. Full Time Sworn Officers by Race and Gender, Fort Wayne Police Department.

	1990	2002
Total Sworn Officers	307	380
White Male	224	275
White Female	18	31
Black Male	41	42
Black Female	13	10
Hispanic Male	9	13
Hispanic Female	1	2
Asian Male	0	2
Asian Female	0	1
Indian Male	1	4
Indian Female	0	0

Source: U.S. Bureau of Justice Statistics, LEMAS, 1990 (computer file), and 2002 unpublished Fort Wayne PD manpower report.

Black male proportion of the total number of sworn officers declined from 13.4% to 11.1%. The actual

Figure 8. Percent of Index Offense Arrests by Age, Fort Wayne 2001.

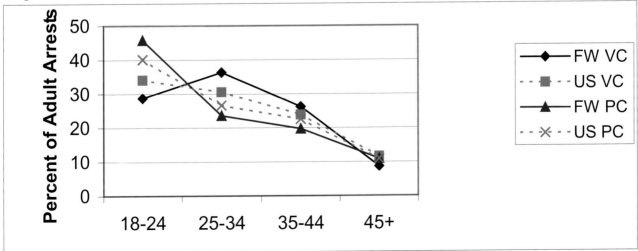

Source: Compiled from Fort Wayne Police Department unpublished data and Federal Bureau of Investigation, Crime in the United States, 2001.

number of Black female sworn officers declined from 13 in 1990 to 10 in 2002. Thus, the proportion of male and female Black sworn officers combined declined from 17.6% of the total in 1990 to 13.7% of the total in 2002. The number of male Hispanic sworn officers increased from 9% to 13% between 1990 and 2002, whereas the number of female Hispanic Officers doubled from 1 to 2 during the twelve- year period. In 1990, Asians and Native Americans were virtually un-represented among sworn officers. By 2002, there were 2 Asian males and 1 Asian female sworn officer, and the number of Native American male sworn officers increased from 1 to 4. There remain no Native American females on the police force. Therefore, although the percentage of traditional White male officers remained the same from 1990 to 2002 and the percentage of Black officers of both genders declined slightly, the police force became somewhat more diverse in terms of non-Black minorities and women.

ALLEN COUNTY JAIL

This section discusses the race and age breakdowns of prisoners processed into the Allen County lockup. In both 2000 and 2001 there were approximately 16,000 inmates processed into the county lockup (Allen County Sheriff's Office unpublished data). Figure 9 shows the percentage of inmates processed into the Allen County Lockup and national jail populations broken

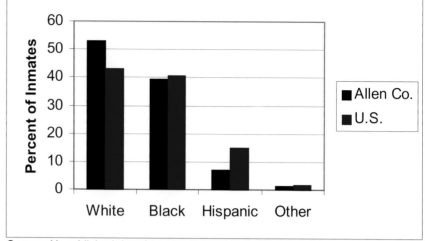

Figure 9. Percent of Inmates Processed Into Allen County Jail Lockup and National Jail Populations by Race/ Ethnicity, 2000-2001.

Source: Unpublished data from the Allen County Sheriff's Office and Prison and Jail Inmates at Midyear 2001.

down by race in 2001. In Fort Wayne, Whites accounted for approximately 50% of the inmates processed, Blacks accounted for around 40%, Hispanics less than 10%, and other racial/ethnic categories represented less than 1% of inmates processed. Nationally in 2001, about 43% of jail inmates were white, 41% were African- American, 15% were Hispanic, and about 2% were other race/ethnic categories (Beck, Allen J., Jennifer C. Karberg, and Paige M. Harrison, Prison and Jail Inmates at Midyear 2001, Table 1, US. Dept of Justice, Washington, DC: USGPO). Therefore, racial/ ethnic

breakdowns of prisoners processed into the Allen County lockup prisoners are relatively similar to national averages, with the exception that the percent of Hispanic inmates is lower in Allen County and the percent of White inmates is higher than the national average.

Figure 10 shows the age breakdown of inmates processed into the Allen County lockup in 2000 and 2001. Consistent with the arrest statistics discussed earlier, persons under 40 years of age accounted for approximately 80% of inmates processed into the county lockup. For

Figure 10. Percent of Inmates Processed Into Allen County Lockup By Age, 2000- 2001.

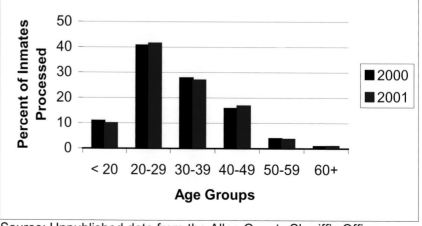

Source: Unpublished data from the Allen County Sheriff's Office.

adults over the age of 20 the likelihood of going to the county lockup consistently declined with age in Allen County. Inmates between the ages of 20 and 40 accounted for approximately two thirds of the inmates processed in 2000 and 2001. Approximately 40% of the inmates in both 2000 and 2001 were between the ages of 20 and 29.

CITIZEN COMPLAINTS

This section discusses complaints filed in the City of Fort Wayne Indiana Citizens' Contact Office (CCO) against the Fort Wayne Police Department in 2000-01 and 2001-02. The office was created in 2000. The stated goal of the office is… "to provide an impartial process for review of citizen's complaints of misconduct by the Fort Wayne Police officers within a non threatening environment (unpublished 1st Annual Report 2000-2001 City of Fort Wayne Indiana Citizen's Contact Office, 2001, p.i)." The rest of this section describes the kinds of citizen complaints filed against Fort Wayne police officers, the disposition of those complaints, and the race and gender of citizen complainants.

The Citizens Contact office received 861 citizen contacts, which generated 139 complaints from April 2000 to April 2001. During the same 12-month period from May 2001 to April 2002, the office received 801 contacts, which generated 114 complaints. The low number of complaints in relation to citizen contacts is due to the nature of the calls the office receives. Frequently, citizens will call with requests for information or call

Table 2. Percent of Citizen Complaints by Type.

Complaint Type	2000-01	2001-02
Verbal Abuse	28	22
Excessive Force	27	17
Harassment	20	18
False Arrest	15	
Illegal Entry		11
Destruction of Property		17
Conduct Unbecoming		15
Other	10	

Source: Unpublished 2000-2001, 2001-2002 Annual Reports of the Fort Wayne Citizen Complaint Contact Office.

regarding issues that are best handled by another office (e.g. traffic complaints). In other situations the citizen simply wishes to report some activity without following through on a formal complaint or the citizen realizes that the police followed proper procedures after conferring with the contact officer (p.3, 2000-2001 Citizen's Contact Office Annual Report). Once the complaint has been completed and signed, it is forwarded to the Internal Affairs division of the Fort Wayne PD for investigation. Table 2 shows a breakdown of the percentage of complaints filed by type. In 2000-2001, 28% of the complaints were for verbal abuse, 27% for excessive force, 20% for harassment, 15% for false arrest and 10% for other types of complaints. In 2001-2002, 22% of the total were for verbal abuse, 17% for excessive force, 18% for harassment, 11% for illegal entry, 17% for destruction of property, and 15% for conduct unbecoming an officer. It is encouraging to see that the number of complaints went down by nearly 20%. It is also encouraging to see that the percentage of complaints for verbal abuse, excessive force and harassment dropped from

75% of the total to 55% of the total complaints against police officers. However, the Citizen's Contact office has existed for only two years and a longer period of study will be needed to draw sound conclusions regarding trends.

Citizen complaints can be disposed of in one of four ways by Fort Wayne PD's Internal Affairs (IA) division. Cases are determined to be unfounded when the allegations are deemed to be true but do not support any charges. Complaints are unsustained when there is no probable cause found to support a charge. A charge is sustained when there is probable cause to believe that police misconduct has occurred. The complaint is then forwarded to the Chief of Police for further action. Table 3 describes the disposition of complaints for the 2000-2001 and 2001-2002

Table 3. Percent of Citizen Complaints by Disposition.

Disposition	2000-01	2001-02
Unsustained	60	49
Sustained	7	4
Unfounded	1	5
Pending	32	42

Source: Unpublished 2000-2001, 2001-2002 Annual Reports of the Fort Wayne Citizen Complaint Contact Office.

reporting years. In the 2000 reporting year 61% of complaints were determined to be unsustained or unfounded. Only 7% were sustained. However, at the time of the report, 32% of complaints were still pending. Therefore, it is important to be cautious about any conclusions. The percent of sustained complaints dropped to 4% in the 2001-2002 reporting year but

42% of cases were still pending as of the time of the report.

Figure 11 shows the race/ ethnicity of citizen complainants in the 2000-2001 and 2001-2002 reporting years. In both years approximately 40% of complainants were White, and more than 50% were African-American. Persons of Hispanic origin and other racial backgrounds made up less than 10% of complainants in both years.

Figure 12 shows the percentage of complaints broken down by gender for the 2000-2001 and 2001-2002 reporting years. In both reporting years, the majority of citizen complaints were from men. In the 2000-2001 reporting year, 60% of complainants were men. In the 2001-2002 reporting year that figured dropped slightly to 57%. Since the majority of arrests involve male suspects (see earlier discussion), it is somewhat surprising that females make up such a large percentage of complainants. It would be interesting to know if the type of

complaint varies by gender. For example, it could be that females complain more for verbal abuse or harassment and males complain more for excessive force. Knowing whether types of complaints vary by gender would be useful in determining the nature/extent of gender related issues in police misconduct. It is also important not to draw too many conclusions from only two years of data on citizen complaints.

BIAS CRIMES

This section discusses incidents of bias or hate crimes. In 1990 Congress first defined hate or bias crimes as those that are, ... "motivated by a bias against a person's race, religion, sexual orientation, or ethnicity/national origin (Federal Bureau of Investigation, p.5, Hate Crime Statistics, 2000, http://www.fbi.gov/ucr/cius_00/hate00.pdf)." Disability was added to the list of bias motivations in 1994. Nationally there were more than 9,000 bias crime incidents in 2000, which was the latest year for which information was available (Federal Bureau of Investigation, p.5, Hate Crime Statistics, 2000, http://www.fbi.gov/ucr/cius_00/hate00.pdf). In 2001, the Fort Wayne Police Department reported 15 bias crime incidents (unpublished Indiana State Police Bias Crime Report, 2001). Figure 13 shows a breakdown of the percentage of crimes in Fort Wayne in 2001 and the national averages in 2000 by bias motivation. Overall the percentages of crimes reported in Fort Wayne track the

Figure 11. Percent of Citizen Complaints by Race of Complainant, Fort Wayne PD, 2000-2002.

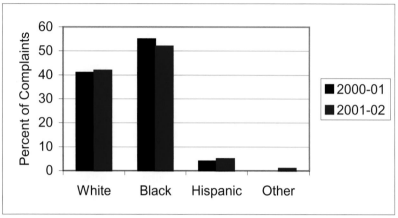

Source: Unpublished 2000-2001, 2001-2002 Annual Reports of the Fort Wayne Citizen Complaint Contact Office.

Figure 12. Percent of Citizen Complaints by Gender of Complainant, Fort Wayne PD, 2000-02.

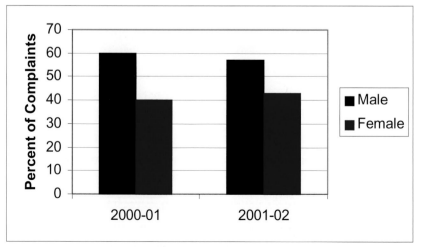

Source: Unpublished 2000-2001, 2001-2002 Annual Reports of the Fort Wayne Citizen Complaint Contact Office.

Figure 13. Percent of Bias Crimes By Motivation, Fort Wayne PD 2001, and United States, 2000.

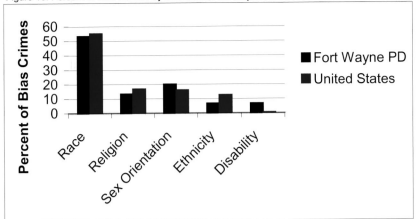

Source: Unpublished Indiana State Police Bias Crime Report 2001 and FBI, Hate Crime Statistics, 2001.

national averages very closely. Approximately 50% were based on racial bias, 10% were based on religion, 20% were based on sexual orientation, and less than 10% were based on ethnicity or disability. It is important to keep in mind that the figures only represent one year's data and only a small number of incidents. Therefore, small changes in the number of offenses in a particular category could mean large percentage changes. In addition, it is often difficult to determine the underlying motivation for crimes because no one witnessed them or the motivation is not immediately apparent (Federal Bureau of Investigation, Hate Crime Statistics, 2000, http://www.fbi.gov/ucr/cius_00/hate00.pdf). Therefore, some portion of hate crimes go undetected or are not labeled as hate crimes by police.

DATA NOT CURRENTLY BEING COLLECTED

This section briefly discusses some information that would be beneficial for tracking issues of race and ethnicity in Fort Wayne criminal justice but is not currently available. One type of information that would be very beneficial is information on the race and gender of offenders charged, convicted, and sentenced through the Allen County court system. This information is not currently available in any easily accessible form. In the existing system, one would have to follow up on each case individually in order to determine the kind of sentence that is administered for each offense. Ideally, it would be beneficial to know the average sentence length for various offenses and whether this varies by race, once other relevant factors such as the relationship of the offender and victim, the offender's

criminal history, employment status, and age have been controlled. This is the only effective way to determine if race plays a role in sentencing. Therefore, updating the Allen County court case processing computers to track cases and dispositions by individual offender characteristics would be very beneficial.

In addition, as noted above, it would be desirable to determine whether the type of citizen complaint and the disposition of citizen complaints in Fort Wayne are related to race and gender. The citizen complaint information discussed above showed that complaints were disproportionately likely to be filed by women and African-Americans. The next step in this process is to determine why this is the case. This would probably take an in-depth study to find general patterns of characteristics across individual complaints.

Chapter 8: Health

C.K. Chauhan, Ph.D.

INTRODUCTION

This chapter discusses several aspects of health issues that afflict the African-American community in the state of Indiana, specifically in Allen County. The topics mentioned are as follows: top seven leading causes of deaths among African-Americans, other pertinent health issues such as HIV/AIDS, infant mortality, obesity, and the economics of health disparity. The descriptive statistics of subjects' gender and race are included and the county statistics are compared with those of state and national.

LEADING CAUSES OF DEATHS IN ALLEN COUNTY

Heart disease and cancer were the top two leading causes of deaths for Whites as well as for African-Americans for Allen County from 1995-1999. The data shows that among the Whites 32% of the deaths were due to heart disease and 25% were due to cancer. Among African-Americans, 25% of the deaths were due to cancer, and 23% were due to heart disease. Among the Allen county population, the percentage of deaths due to heart disease and cancer were 31% and 25% respectively (2001 Minority Healthy report). African-Americans in Indiana have a higher mortality rate in heart disease (243.5 per 100,000) than among any other race. This rate, however, is lower than the national rate of 267.8.

In 2000, 37% of the deaths among Blacks in Allen County were due to heart disease. This is a significant increase from 23% in past years. In table 4 there was a 6% increase of deaths due to heart disease among

KEY FINDINGS

- Heart disease and cancer are the top two leading causes of death for both Whites and African-Americans.

- Among African-Americans the percentage of deaths due to heart disease is on the rise. The percentage of deaths among African-Americans due to stroke are also on the rise.

- Of those African-Americans who died of diabetes in 2000, eighty percent were women. However, of those African-Americans who died of homicide during the same year, eighty nine percent were males.

- More than two thirds of adult men and about one half of adult women are either overweight or obese. (It is important to note that the data on obesity was obtained by a telephone survey and may have the risk of inaccuracy due to inaccurate reporting.

- The infant mortality and the neonatal death rates among African-Americans are significantly higher than those of Whites in Allen County.

Table 1. Leading Causes of Death for Caucasians in Allen County 1995 - 1999

Rank Cause of Death	White
1 Heart disease	3,631
2 Malignant neoplasms	2,845
3 Cerebrovascular disease	770
4 COPD/CLRD	538
5 Accidents and adverse effects	501
6 Pneumonia and influenza	305
7 Diabetes	290
8 Nephritis, nephrotic syndrome, and nephrosis	223
9 Suicide	142
10 Alzheimers	136
Total	11,323

Source: 2001 Minority Health Report

Table 2. Leading Causes of Death for African-Americans in Allen County 1995 - 1999

Rank Cause of Death	Black
1 Malignant neoplasms	301
2 Heart disease	281
3 Cerebrovascular disease	69
3 Accidents and adverse effects	69
3 Homicide	69
6 Diabetes	64
7 Nephritis, nephrotic syndrome, and nephrosis	32
8 Certain conditions originating in the perinatal period	31
9 Pneumonia and influenza	27
10 COPD/CLRD	25
Total	1,213

Source: 2001 Minority Health Report

Whites in 2000. There was no significant change in the percentage of deaths due to cancer for Blacks as well as for White. In 2000; African-American women accounted for 56% of the deaths among Blacks due to cancer.

Table 3: Causes of death for Blacks in Allen County, 2000
Total Number of deaths: **261**

Cancer	Males: 27	Females: 27	Total 61 =23.4%
Heart Disease	Males: 47	Females: 50	Total 97 =37.2%
Strokes	Males: 9	Females: 11	Total 20 =7.7%
Accidents	Males: 3	Females: 3	Total 6=2.3%
Homicide	Males: 9	Females: 1	Total 9=3.4%
Diabetes	Males: 2	Females: 8	Total 10=3.8%
Suicide	Males: 2	Females: 1	Total 3=1.1%

Source: Indiana Mortality Report, 2000

Table 4: Causes of death for Caucasians in Allen County, 2000
Total Number of deaths, **2296**

Cancer	Males: 294	Females: 255	Total 549 =23.9%
Heart Disease	Males: 447	Females: 434	Total 881 =33.4%
Strokes	Males: 60	Females: 84	Total 144 =6.3%
Accidents	Males: 33	Females: 34	Total 67=2.9%
Homicide	Males: 8	Females: 2	Total 10=0.4%
Diabetes	Males: 28	Females: 34	Total 62=2.7%
Suicide	Males: 17	Females: 5	Total 22=1.0%

Source: Indiana Mortality Report, 2000

Strokes, accidents, and homicide were tied for the third leading causes of death for African-Americans in Allen County between the years of 1995-1999. Table 2 shows that 5.7% of the deaths were due to each of these causes. The percentage of deaths due to stroke for Whites in Allen County in 1995-1999 was 6.8%. According to the American Stroke Association Statistics (1999), African-Americans have a higher stroke rate than any other racial group, (87.4 per 100,000 for men and 78.1 per 100,000 for women). In year 2000, stroke accounted for 7.7% of deaths for African-Americans in Allen County in 2000, a 2% increase from past years. However, for the White population this percentage was 6.3% for year 2000, slightly down from the percent of past years. Tables 3 and 4 also show that for the same year African Americans in Allen County were nine times more likely to die from homicide than their White counterparts. Men accounted for 84% of the homicides

in Allen County. Of the 9 African-American homicides in 2000, eight were men.

Diabetes was the next leading (sixth in rank) cause of death for African Americans in Allen County, 1995-1999, claiming 5.3% of the deaths. This percentage fell to 3.8% in 2000. However, in the same year 80% of these deaths were among women. Among Whites, 2.6% of deaths in

Allen County during 1995-1999 were due to diabetes, which rose to 2.7% in 2000. Of the 62 deaths occurring among the White residents in this period, 54 % were women.

The 2001 Minority Health Report shows that in 1999, African Americans in Indiana have a significantly higher rate of diabetes (58.7 per 100,000) than their White counterparts (25.4 per 1000,000). This rate for African-Americans is also significantly higher than the Indiana rate as well as the national rate.

HIV/AIDS

According to Indiana State Department of Health HIV/STD Quarterly Report, 2002, Allen County has 316 people(83% males and 17% females) living with HIV, of which 202 are Whites and 92 are Blacks. It is important to understand that Indiana is one of the 34 states that separately reports the number of cases that

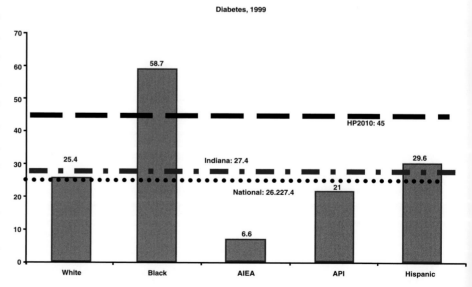

Diabetes, 1999

* Numbers vary due to population of race or ethnic group being compared
* Race and Ethnic groups are based on Indiana's Mortality Rate 1999
* Rates are per 100,000 population
* Total death numbers that are below 20 are not statistically sound
* Hispanic is an ethnicity and it includes all races.

[5] National Institute of Diabetes & Digestive & Kidney Disease

Table 5
Cumulative Cases Through September 30, 2001 - Indiana HIV/AIDS
Cumulative Cases Through December 2000 - U.S. AIDS

Race	Indiana HIV				Indiana AIDS				U.S. AIDS*			
	Male	%	Female	%	Male	%	Female	%	Male	%	Female	%
White	1,836	62%	349	50%	4,111	73%	370	54%	302,323	48%	28,834	22%
Black	985	33%	324	46%	1,353	24%	284	42%	214,898	33%	77,624	58%
Hispanic	124	4%	24	3%	178	3%	21	3%	115,069	18%	26,625	20%
Other	15	1%	3	0.31%	15	0.22%	5	1%	6,894	1%	1,170	1%
Total									639,184			
with missing race	2,961	100%		100%		100%		100%	640,022	100%	134,441	100%

Source: Indiana State Department of Health

Table 6
Cumulative Cases Through September 30, 2002 - Indiana HIV/AIDS
Cumulative Cases Through December 2001 - U.S. AIDS

Race	Indiana HIV				Indiana AIDS				U.S. AIDS*			
	Male	%	Female	%	Male	%	Female	%	Male	%	Female	%
White	1,948	62%	371	48%	4,339	72%	417	54%	313,034	47%	30,854	21%
Black	1,030	33%	364	47%	1,489	25%	328	42%	228,499	34%	84,681	58%
Hispanic	136	4%	27	4%	205	3%	27	3%	121,198	18%	28,554	20%
Other	21	1%	4	1%	16	0%	4	1%	7,956	1%	1,372	1%
Total with missing race	3,135	100%	766	100%	6,049	100%	776	100%	670,687	100%	145,461	100%

* Includes 545 males and 89 females whose race is unknown
** Includes 1 person whose sex is unknown / Source: Indiana State Department of Health

progress from an HIV status to a full stage of AIDS.

Table 6 shows that through September 2002 in Indiana, White males accounted for 62% of the HIV cases and Black males accounted for 33% of the HIV cases among men. Among females, however, White and Blacks accounted for 48% and 47% HIV cases, respectively. Those diagnosed with AIDS virus were as follows: among males, 72% Whites and 25% Blacks; among females, 54% Whites and 25% Blacks. In comparison Table 5 reveals an increase in the number of HIV and AIDS reported cases from 2001 to 2002. It is important to understand that the increase in the number of reported cases does not necessarily imply the rise in the incidences of the diseases.

OBESITY

According to Indiana State Department of Health, an estimated 40.3% of adult males and 26.7% of adult females in Allen County were overweight in 2001. An additional 27.9% of males and 21% of females were obese. In other words an estimated 68.2% of adult men and an estimated 47.7% of adult women were considered overweight or obese.

The source, Indiana Behavioral Risk Factor Surveillance System (IBRFSS), is a telephone survey relying on self-reported data and therefore may have the risk of inaccuracy due to under-reporting behaviors that may be considered undesirable. The graph shows an upward trend in the percentage of obese cases among Blacks in Indiana from 1995-1998, with the highest at about 32% in 1998. From 1996-1999 the percentage of obese among African-Americans was higher than that of Whites. IBRFSS also reported that a higher percentage of African-American respondents were overweight compared to White respondents. The respondents in the higher income bracket were the least likely to be obese, but there was not a big difference between the education levels for the respondents that are overweight or obese (Indiana State Department Of Health).

INFANT MORTALITY

Between 1991 and 2000, an average of 5,047 births occurred per year in Allen county with 5,213 births in 2000. The 2001 Minority Health Report uses the following definitions: Infant mortality is

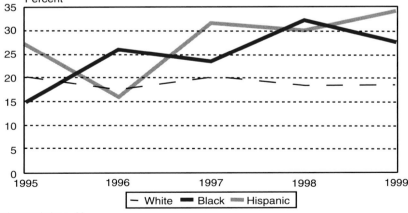

Obese* by Race
Indiana Residents, 1995-1999

*Body mass index >=30
Source: Indiana Behavioral Risk Factor Surveillance System

Table 7. Infant, Neonatal, and Postneonatal Mortality for Allen County, 2000.

	Live Births	Infant Deaths	Neonatal Deaths	Post-Neonatal
All	5,213	32	20	12
White	4,327	18	10	8
Black	743	11	9	2

Source: Infant, Neonatal, Postneonatal Mortality Report, Indiana Residents, 2000

defined as those deaths that occur within the first year of life. Neonatal mortality is defined as those deaths that occur within the first 28 days of life, and Postneonatal are those deaths that occur after the first 28 days but before the age of one. Table 7 reveals that in Allen County the infant mortality rate (IMR) was 4.1 per 1,000 live births for Whites and 14.8 per 1,000 live births for African-Americans in year 2000. The African American IMR in Indiana is 17.0 per 1,000 live births. Incidentally, the national rate for African-Americans is highest, at 14.6 per 1,000 live births, while the national average is 7.1 per 1,000 live births. (Indiana State Department of Health).

POSTNEONATAL AND NEONATAL MORTALITY RATES

In Allen County the Postneonatal rate for African Americans was 2.7 per 1,0000 live births as compared to 1.9 per 1,000 live births for the whites. However there is a significant difference when looking at the Neonatal rate, which is 12.1 per 1,000 live births for African-Americans as compared to 2.3 per 1,000 live births for the Whites.

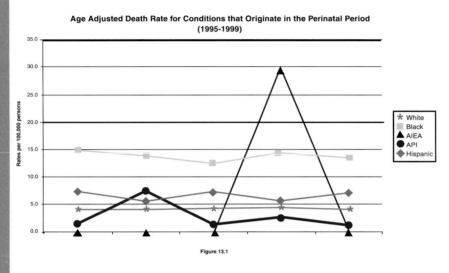

Figure 13.1

ECONOMICS OF HEALTH DISPARITIES

Author: Elizabeth L. Hamilton-Byrd, MD

The Economics of health disparities is important information and data to review. This may often explain the reasoning behind many of the morbidity and mortality that exists throughout the communities in Indiana. Dr. Elizabeth Hamilton from The Office of Minority Health Report 2001, provides a brief description of what some of these health disparities may be in Indiana.

Using 1999 Indiana Hospital Discharge Data to calculate total inpatient charges for the leading chronic diseases and age-adjusted* mortality rates for Indiana for 2000 to calculate the disparity between the White population and the Black population, we can obtain a very rough estimate of some of the costs of health disparities in Indiana.

From the 2000 Census, Black or African Americans comprise 8.4% of the Indiana population. Some examples of the top leading causes of death plaguing the Black population are:
heart disease, cancer, cerebrovascular diseases (predominantly stroke), and diabetes mellitus.

Heart Disease

Black mortality 323.74/100,000
White mortality 270.27/100,000
Ratio of Black to White = 1.20 or a 20% excess mortality in Blacks.

Total inpatient charges for heart disease = $1,379,849,079.45

.084 x $1,379,849,079.45 = $115,907,322.60 expected charges for black patients
$115,907,322.60 x 1.20 = $139,088,787.10 estimated total charges for Black patients based on known disease disparity
$139,088,787.10 - $115,907,322.60 = $23,181,464.52 excess inpatient hospital charges due to health disparity in heart disease

Cancer

Black mortality 262.89/100,000
White mortality 213.52/100,000
Ratio of Black to White = 1.23 or a 23% excess mortality in Blacks
Total inpatient charges for cancer = $408,701,817.32

.084 x $408,701,817.32 = $34,330,952.66 expected charges for black patients
$34,330,952.66 x 1.23 = $42,227,071.76 estimated total charges for Black patients based on known disease disparity
$42,227,071.76 - $34,330,952.66 = $7,896,119.10 excess inpatient hospital charges due to health disparity in cancer

Cerebrovascular disease

Black mortality 86.55/100,000

White mortality 70.39/100,000
Ratio of Black to White = 1.23 or a 23% excess mortality in Blacks 67
Total inpatient charges for cerebrovascular disease = $247,447,095.86
.084 x $247,447,095.86 = $20,785,556.05 expected charges for Black patients
$20,785,556.05 x 1.23 = $25,566,233.94 estimated total charges for Black patients based on known disease disparity
$25,566,233.94 - $20,785,556.05 = $4,780,677.89 excess inpatient hospital charges due to health disparity in cerebrovascular disease

Diabetes mellitus

Black mortality 54.54/100,000
White mortality 26.57/100,000
Ratio of Black to White = 2.05 or a 105% excess mortality in Blacks
Total inpatient charges for diabetes = $87,640,704.10
.084 x $87,640,704.10 = $7,361,819.14 expected charges for Black patients
$7,361,819.14 x 2.05 = $15,091,729.25 estimated total charges for Black patients based on known disease disparity
$15,091,729.25 - $7,361,819.14 = $7,729,910.11 excess inpatient hospital charges due to health disparity in diabetes

Note: The excess burden of disease in Blacks for stroke and diabetes based on mortality rates agreesfairly well with calculations based on the self-reported prevalence in the Indiana 2000 BRFSS.(Stroke: Blacks 3.1%, Whites 2.5%, ratio B/W = 1.24 and Diabetes: Blacks 13.0%, Whites 5.7%,ratio B/W = 2.28)The excess cost figures assume equal hospitalization rates and equal amount and types of treatments for Blacks as for Whites, which we know is not the case. Therefore, these are only very rough estimates of the excess health care costs due to disparities. These calculations are based on those of Kevin Sherin, MD, MPH.

Annotated Bibliographies

Demographics

United States Bureau of the Census Summary Tape File 3, http://factfinder.census.gov/servlet/BasicFactsServlet.

Housing

Association of Community Organizations for Reform Now (ACORN). (2002). *The Great Divide: Home Purchase Mortgage Lending Nationally and in 68 Metropolitan Areas*. http://www.acorn.org/acorn10/communityreinvestment/reports/ HMDA2002/main.htm. Retrieved April, 2003 from ACORN website.

The ACORN study finds Fort Wayne as leading the nation in the percent increase of rejections of African-Americans in the conventional home loan application process. The 36.7 percent increase from 2000 to 2001 indicates a serious issue for African-Americans in Fort Wayne, particularly aspiring homeowners. The largest Latino denial rate percent increase for the same time period is also seen in Fort Wayne.

Anon. (n.d.) *Fort Wayne, Indiana: The City of Commercial and Industrial Opportunities*. Publisher Unknown.

Early booster document (ca. 1929) detailing the positive aspects for potential companies/ people looking to relocate in the area. Housing stock not listed as an attractor.

Bluestone, Barry and Bennett Harrison. (1987). *The Great U-Turn*. NY: Basic Books.

From the authors that defined the changing US economy as one of deindustrialization, they examine the changing focus of the economy to service-sector job creation and how the decline in manufacturing has impacted the urban Midwest and Northeast. Strict focus on economic trends.

Dudley, Kathleen. (1994). *The End of the Line: Lost Jobs, New Lives in Postindustrial America*. Chicago: University of Chicago Press.

An in-depth case study of a 'rust belt' town heavily dependent upon industrial production. Kenosha, Wisconsin was primarily a one company town dependent upon automobile production. The study of how this city coped with plant closings, and still struggles with defining its economic niche in the current economy, is useful in explaining the depth of the impact of deindustrialization on mid-size urban communities.

City of Fort Wayne. Planning Department. (2002). *GIS Maps of Fort Wayne Housing Statistics*. Fort Wayne, IN.

The Alliance Fort Wayne-Allen County Economic Development Alliance. (2003). *2000 Census Data: Demographics*. http://www.theallianceonline.com/page_1.html. Retrieved April 2002 from the Alliance.

Census data for Fort Wayne and Allen County. The Alliance is a private, non-profit organization charged with creating and retaining quality jobs for local residents through the strengthening of existing employers and the attraction of new employers.

S.B. Friedman and Company. (2001). *City of Fort Wayne: Housing Market Study and Development Strategy*. Submitted to City of Fort Wayne, Department of Redevelopment. Chicago: S.B. Friedman and Company.

A survey of housing trends and projections in the Fort Wayne Metropolitan area with special emphasis on Southeast section of town. Results of Allen County housing preference survey and windshield survey of Southeast area. Provides data on sales trends, owner/rental rates, quality of rental stock, and new and resale trends. Key implementation strategies include 1. enhance and market the image and livability of city, 2. invest in neighborhoods, 3. facilitate the redevelopment of vacant land, 4. encourage and facilitate the rehabilitation of existing homes, 5. support new and substantial rehabilitation with shallow income-linked subsidy programs, 6. support and enhance homeownership opportunities, and 7. targe t opportunities for affordable housing.

Indiana State Government. (2002). *Economic Overview*. http://www.in.gov/doc/doingbiz/ econAndWorkPro.html. Retrieved May 2002 from Indiana State Government website.

Basic statistics on the state-level regarding employment and workforce, economy, demographic, and other census data. STATS Indiana is an information service of the Indiana Business Research Center at Indiana University's Kelley School of Business and receives major support from the State of Indiana through the Indiana Department of Commerce.

Massey, Douglas and Nancy Denton. (1993). *American Apartheid: Segregation and the Making of the Underclass*. Boston: Harvard University Press.

Definitive source on the persistence of racial segregation in housing. Argues that residential segregation is the main cause of the limited life chances of African Americans residing in inner city America. The authors find post-WWII segregation levels to the time of writing the highest they have ever been in the history of the nation. Analysis based on the thirty metropolitan cities with the largest total African-American population. Fort Wayne not analyzed, Gary and Indianapolis included in analysis.

Medoff, Harry and Holly Sklar. (1994). *Streets of Hope: The Fall and Rise of an Urban Neighborhood*. Boston: South End Press.

A study of the Dudley Street neighborhood initiative in Boston. One of most successful examples of how inner city residents can take control of their neighborhood and change it for the better, the focus is how disinvestment, segregation, persistent poverty, and urban blight can be overcome by local control and autonomous, democratic decision making.

Lewis Mumford Center for Comparative Urban and Regional Research. (2003). *Metropolitan Racial and Ethnic Change Initiative*. http://www.albany.edu/ mumford/census/index.html. Retrieved April 2003 from Mumford Center at SUNY-Albany.

Complete lists and searchable databases of racial segregation statistics. Data on residential and educational segregation available. Data based on U.S. Census figures.

Sassen, Saskia. (2000). Cities in the World Economy. Thousand Oaks, CA: Pine Forge Press.

An accessible overview of globalization and its impact on local economies. Specific focus on financial and insurance sectors alludes to concentration of wealth and profit and up until very recently, Fort Wayne's prominence among insurance company holdings.

Annotated Bibliographies

Employment

Abt Associates, Inc. (1998, February). The Indiana welfare reform evaluation: Program implementation and economic impacts after two years. Cambridge, MA: Author.

Johnson, G.J. (1989). Underemployment and household livelihood strategies among African Americans. Athens, GA: University of Georgia

Schrock, G. (1998, September). Estimating a basic needs budget for Indiana families. Indianapolis, IN: Indiana Economic Development Council, Inc.

United States Census Bureau (2000). United States Census. Washington, D.C.

Warren, C. Pathways to a liviable Wage: A report for the Indiana Economic Development Council, Inc. May 2001, Indianapolis

Poverty and Welfare

Family Resource Coalition of America Report Winter 1998-99 Vol 17, No.4.

Family Social Service Association, 2003

Indiana Economic Development Council (IEDC), A think tank and consultant for the state on economic development issues, 1998.

Midwest Partners, This organization advocates for poverty reduction and economic self-sufficiency, 2001. www./midwest partners.org

Midwest Welfare Peer Assistance Network, 2000.

Street, Paul (1997). Midwest Job Gap Project, The Recent History and Future of Welfare Reform in Six Midwestern States, Office of Social Policy Research at Northern Illinois University.

The New York Times Magazine, August 18, 1996/Section 6

US Census Bureau: Indiana Business Research Center, 2002.

Business & Economic Development

Dolinsky, Caputo, & Rasumarty, (1984). Long term entrepreneurship patterns: A national study of black and white female entry and stayer status differences. Journal of Small Business Management, pp.18-26.

Humphreys, J. M. African-American buying power by place of residence: 1990-1999. The University of Georgia Terry College of Business, Selig Center for Economic Growth.

Indiana State Chamber of Commerce. (2001). Population estimates by race in Indiana and Fort Wayne.

Lownes-Jackson, M. (2000, January). Flying solo. Black Enterprise [Online]. <http://www.blackenterprise.com>[2/12/03].

Small Business Administration, Office of Advocacy, 1999.

Sonfield M. C. (1986). An exploratory analysis of the largest black-owned U.S. companies." Journal of Small Business Management, 9-17.

United States Department of Labor, Bureau of Labor Statistics (2002). Consumer price index. Washington, D.C.

United States Department of Labor, Bureau of Labor Statistics, Division of Consumer Expenditure Surveys, Office of Prices and Living Conditions. The consumer expenditure survey, 1999. Washington,. D.C.

United States Census Bureau Economic Census (1977). Minority- and women-owned business enterprises. Washington, D.C.

Education

The Advancement Project and The Civil Rights Project. (2000). <u>Opportunities suspended: The devastating consequences of zero tolerance and school discipline policies.</u> [Online]. Harvard University, The Civil Rights Project. <<u>http://www.civilrightsproject.harvard.edu/convenings/zerotolerance/ call_synopsis.php.</u>> [2003, Jan 22]. Ansell, S.E. & McCabe, M. (2003). Quality counts 2003: The teacher gap, off target. <u>Education Week, 22</u> (17), 57-58.

Boggs, W. R. (1993). Racial differences—why they matter. *American Renaissance* [Online], *4*:1. <<u>http://www.amren.com/931issue/931issue.html</u>> [2003, Jan. 3].

Chaika, G. (2001). Recruiting and retaining minority teachers: Programs that work! *Education World* [Online],<<u>http://www.educationworld.com/a_admin/admin213.shtml</u>>[2002, Dec. 10].

Delgado, G. (1999, Spring). Race and regionalism. <u>GRIPP News and Notes 1</u> [Online]. <<u>http://www.arc.org/gripp/researchPublications/newsletter/vol1spring99/newsVol1Spring99.html</u>> [2003, Jan. 3].

<u>Exclusion from school and racial equality: A good practice guide</u>. 1997. London, UK: The Commission for Racial Equality. Ferguson, R. F. (1998). Teachers' perceptions and expectations and the black-white test score gap. In C. Jenks & M. Phillips (Eds.), <u>The black-white test score gap</u> (pp. 273-317). Washington, DC: Brookings Institution.

Fletcher, M. A. (2002, February 21). Indiana schools shrink black-white divide: A focus on attitudes raises altitudes in scores. <u>The Washington Post</u>, p.A03.

(1999). Fort Wayne Community Schools (FWCS) tell why they have retained Jonamay Lambert & Associates Inc. [Online Brochure]. Jonamay Lambert & Associates. <<u>http://www.lambert-diversity.com/PDF/1999_Spring.pdf</u>>[January 13, 2003].

Frankenberg, E., Lee, C., & Orfield, G. (2003). A multiracial society with segregated schools: Are we losing the dream? [Online]. The Harvard University Civil Rights Project. <<u>http://www.civilrightsproject.harvard.edu/research/reseg03/AreWeLosingtheDream.pdf</u>> [January 9, 2003].

Fritzberg, G. (2001). From rhetoric to reality: Opportunity-to-learn standards and the integrity of American public school reform. <u>Teacher Education Quarterly, 28</u> (1), 169-187.

Fritzberg, G. (1999). <u>In the shadow of excellence: Recovering a vision of educational opportunity for all</u>. San Francisco: Caddo Gap Press.

Greer-Chase, M., Rhodes, W., Kellam, S.G., & Gruss, M. (2002). Why the prevention of aggressive disruptive behaviors in middle school must begin in elementary school. <u>Clearing House, 75</u> (5), 242-247.

Gruss, M. & Shawgo, R. (2001, March 11). Segregation still a fact in a diverse city, p. A1.

Hanushek, E. A., Kain, J. F., & Rivkin, S. G. (2002). <u>New evidence about Brown v. Board of Education: The complex effects of school racial composition on achievement</u>. (Working Paper No. 8741, pp. 1-9, 29-30). National Bureau of Economic Research.

Haycock, K. (2002). State policy levers: Closing the achievement gap. <u>The State Education Standard, 3</u> 6-13.

Haycock, M. (2001). Closing the achievement gap. <u>Educational Leadership, 58</u> (6), 6-11.

He, W., & Hobbs, F. (1999). <u>The emerging minority marketplace, minority population growth: 1995 to 2050</u>. Washington, DC: U.S. Department of Commerce, Minority Business Development Agency.

How it happened: The desegregation of Fort Wayne, Indiana, schools. (1998). <u>Christian Science Monitor, 54</u> (3).

Jencks, C, & Phillips, M. (1998). America's next achievement test: Closing the black-white test score gap. *The American Prospect* [Online}, *9*: 40. <<u>http://www.prospect.org/print/V9/40/jencks-c.html</u>> [2002, Dec. 10]

Johnston, R. C. & Viadero, D. (2000, March 15). Unmet promise: Raising minority achievement. *Education Week* [Online]. <<u>http://www.edweek.org/ew/ewstory.cfm?slug=27gapintro.h19&keywords=unmet%20promise</u>> [2002, April 2]

Keleher, T. & Johnson, T. (2001). Confronting institutional racism. <u>Leadership, 30</u> (4), 24-26, 38.

Kilmann, R.H., Saxton M.J., & Serpa, R. (1985). Five key issues in understanding and changing culture. In R.H. Kilmann, M.J. Saxton, & R. Serpa (Eds.), Gaining control of corporate culture (pp. 1-16). San Francisco: Jossey-Bass.

Knowles, L.L. & Kenneth Prewitt (Eds.). (1970). Institutional racism in America. Englewood Cliffs, N.J., Prentice-Hall.

Kober, N. (2001). It takes more than testing: Closing the achievement gap. [Online]. Center on Education Policy. <http://www.ctredpol.org/improvingpublicschools/closingachievementgap.pdf.> [2002, April].

Kozol, J. (1991). Savage inequalities: Children in America's schools. New York: Crown Publishing.

Kuykendall, Ed.D., J.D., C. 1991. Improving black student achievement by enhancing student's self-image: The Mid-Atlantic Equity Center

Listening to minority students: One district's approach to closing the achievement gap. In M. Sadowski (Ed.), Adolescents at school: Perspectives on youth, identity, and education, Cambridge, MA: Harvard Education Press.

Losen, D. & Orfield, G. (Eds.) (2002). Racial inequity in special education. Cambridge, MA: Harvard Education Publishing Group.

McAdams, R. P. & Zinck, R.A. (1998, Fall). The power of the superintendent's leadership in shaping school district culture: Three case studies. ERS Spectrum, (3),

McCombs, B. L. (2000). Reducing the achievement gap. Society, 37 (5), 29-37.

National Center for Education Statistics (NCES). (2001). NAEP summary data tables. [Online]. Washington, DC: U.S. Department of Education <http://nces.edu.gov/nationsreportcard> [2003, Jan. 3].

National Education Association (NEA).(2002). Tomorrow's teachers: Help wanted: Minority teachers. [Online]. Washington, DC: National Education Association. <http://www.nea.org/tomorrowsteachers/2002/helpwanted.html.> [2003, Jan. 14].

Neumann, K. (1987). Quantitative and qualitative approaches in educational research-problems and examples of controlled understanding through interpretive methods. International Review of Education, 33 (2), 159-170.

Newell, R. J. (2002). A different look at accountability: The EdVisions approach. Phi Delta Kappan 84 (3), 208-211.

Orfield, G. (2001). Schools more separate: Consequences of a decade of resegregation. Cambridge, MA: Harvard University, The Civil Rights Project.

Ramsey, V. J. & Gallos, J. V. (year). Teaching diversity: Listening to the soul, speaking from the heart. San Francisco: Jossey-Bass.

Rosenthal, L. (2003). What makes a great principal? GreatSchools.net Newsletter [Online]. <http://fortwayne.greatschools.net/cgi-bin/showarticle/IN/18/improve#Great> [2003, Jan. 23].

Sadowski, M. (2001). Closing the gap one school at a time. Harvard Education Letter [Online]. <http://www.edletter.org/past/issues/2001-mj/gap.shtml.> [2002, Aug. 8].

Scott, T. M., Nelson, C. M., & Liaupsin, C.J. (2001). Effective instruction: The forgotten component in preventing school violence. Education & Treatment of Children, 24 (3), 309-322.

Sergiovanni, T.J. (1987). The theoretical basis for cultural leadership. In M.B. Schoenheit & L.T. Sheive (Eds.), Leadership: Examining the elusive (pp. 116-127). Alexandria, VA: Association for Supervision and Curriculum Development.

Shanker, A. (1996). Passing on failure: District promotion policies and practices. Washington, DC: American Federation of Teachers.

Skiba, R. J., Chung, C. G., Wu, T. C., Simmons, A. B., & St. John, E. P. (2000). Minority overrepresentation in Indiana's special education programs: A status report. Bloomington, IN: Indiana Department of Education Division of Special Education.

Spriggs, W. (Ed.) (1999). The state of black America, 1999: The impact of color-consciousness in the United States. New York, NY: National Urban League, Inc.

Starr, L. (1997). Can schools stop promoting failure? *Education World* [Online]. <http://www.education-world.com/a_issues/issues021.shtml.> [2002, Dec. 10].

State of the states. (2003). Education Week, 22 (17), 75-76,78.

The state of black America. (2001). New York, NY: The National Urban League.

Theobald, N. (2001). Indiana's strategy for funding charter schools. Bloomington, IN: Indiana University, Indiana Education Policy Center.

Uhlenberg, J. & Brown, K. M. (2002). Racial gap in teachers' perceptions of the achievement gap. Education and Urban Society, 34 (4), 493-530.

U.S. Department of Education, National Center for Education Statistics (NCES). (1999). Teacher quality: A report on the preparation and qualifications of public school teachers (Office of Educational Research and Improvement NCRS 1999-080). Washington, DC: U.S. Government Printing Office.

Viadero, D. (2000, March 22). Lags in mnority achievement defy traditional explanations. *Education Week* [Online]. <http://www.edweek.org/ew/ewstory.cfm?slug=28causes.h19.> [2003, Jan. 3].

Viadero, D. (2001, September 19). Teachers' race linked to students' scores. *Education Week* [Online]. <http://www.edweek.org/ew/newstory.cfm?slug=03race.h21.> [2003, Jan. 3].

Wenglinsky, H. (2001). Teacher classroom practices and student performance: How schools can make a difference. [Online]. <http://www.ets.org/research/dload/RIBRR-01-19.pdf.> [2002, Aug. 28].

Yasin, S. & Albert, B. (1999). Minority teacher recruitment and retention: A national imperative. Washington, DC: American Association of Colleges for Teacher Education.

Crime and Justice

Allen County Sheriff's Office. (2000-2001). [Annual jail reports]. Unpublished data.

Beck, A.J., Karberg, J.C., & Harrison, P.M. (2002) Prison and jail inmates at midyear 2001 [Table 11]. [Online].[NCJ 191702], [Accessed 7/17/2002], [http://www.ojp.usdoj.gov/bjs/pub/pdf/pjim01.pdf]

Citizen's Contact Office, City of Fort Wayne Indiana. (2001,2002). [Annual Report 2000-2001, 2001-2002]. Unpublished.

Federal Bureau of Investigation. (2000). Crime in the United States, 2000. [Online]. United States Government. http://www.fbi.gov/ucr/cius_00/00crime1.pdf [Accessed 7/15/2002].

Federal Bureau of Investigation. (1985-2000). Crime in the United States. Washington, D.C.: U.S. Government Printing Office.

Federal Bureau of Investigation. (2000). Hate crime statistics, 2000. [Online]. http://www.fbi.gov/ucr/cius_00/hate00.pdf [Accessed 7/16/2002].

Fort Wayne Police Department. (1999-2001). [Arrest data]. Unpublished data.

Fort Wayne Police Department. (2002). [Manpower report]. Unpublished.

Indiana State Police. (2001). [Bias crime report]. Unpublished.

United States Bureau of Justice Statistics. (1990). Law enforcement management and administrative statistics, 1990. [computer file].

United States Census Bureau. (2000). Census of population, 2000. [Online]. <http:/factfinder.census.gov>. [Accessed 7/17/2002].

United States Census Bureau. (1990, 2000). Census of population (1990, 2000). Washington, D.C.: U.S. Government Printing Office.

Health

Indiana Department of Health/Data and Statistics

www.state.in.us/isdh/dataandstats/data_and_statistics.htm

The Indiana Minority Health Report, 2001

http://www.in.gov/isdh/publications/minority/2001

Alex
Tay
Sei
Ayu